GENDER DIMENSIONS

Developing Interpersonal Skills in the Classroom

Andrea Allard
and
Jeni Wilson

ELEANOR CURTAIN
PUBLISHING

Dedication

For Madison and other children of the nineties. May they have the chance to enjoy more equitable, constructive relationships with girls and boys of all races and backgrounds.

Distributed in North America by:
Peguis Publishers
100-318 McDermot Avenue
Winnipeg, MB
Canada R3A 0A2

First published in 1995

ELEANOR CURTAIN PUBLISHING
906 Malvern Road
Armadale 3143
Australia

Copyright © Andrea Allard and Jeni Wilson 1995

All rights reserved. Apart from any fair dealing for the purposes of study, research, criticism or review as permitted under the Copyright Act, no part of this book may be reproduced by any process without permission. Copyright owners may take legal action against a person who infringes their copyright through unauthorised copying. Inquiries should be directed to the publisher.

National Library of Australia CIP

Allard, Andrea, C.
  Gender dimensions: developing interpersonal skills in the classroom.

  ISBN 1 875327 34 7.

  1. Teacher–student relationships. 2. Sex differences in education. 3. Educational equalisation. 4. Sex role in children. 5. Sexism in education. I. Wilson, Jeni. II. Title.

372.11023

Production by Sylvana Scannapiego, Island Graphics
Edited by Ruth Siems
Cover designed by David Constable
Cover photograph, Eastmoor Primary School, by Sara Curtain
Design and page make-up by Patricia Tsiatsias
Printed in Australia by Impact Printing

Contents

Preface	v
Acknowledgements	iv
Part one: Starting Points	1
Introduction to *Gender Dimensions*	2
Elements of a constructive learning environment	7
Active involvement in group building	8
Communication	9
Cooperation	11
Problem-solving and negotiation	13
Beliefs about a constructive learning environment	14
Starting with ourselves: Teachers and change	15
Understanding ourselves	15
Developing new skills: Learning together	16
Part two: Activities	21
Learning area overview grid	22
Activity layout	23
Group building	24
1.1 Terrific Terri name game	26
1.2 Fruit salad	28
1.3 Stomp	30
1.4 What do feelings look like?	32
1.5 Compliment beanbag	34
1.6 Jigsaw people	36
1.7 Characteristics cube	38
Group building: Moving forward	40
Communication	43
2.1 What does listening look like?	48
2.2 Mirroring feelings	52
2.3 Machine Maker	54
2.4 I feel ... when ...	58
2.5 Representing feelings	60

2.6 Accident report	62
2.7 Blackboard target	64
2.8 Talk-up triangle	66
2.9 Two-minute controversial responses	70
2.10 Take two	72
Communication: Moving forward	74

Cooperative learning   80

3.1 Build it together	82
3.2 The Paperbag Princes: story map	84
3.3 Create a slogan	87
3.4 Collective cloze	90
3.5 Jumble and unjumble	92
3.6 Body sculpture	94
3.7 Guess and check	96
3.8. Newspaper reconstruction	98
Cooperation: Moving forward	100

Problem-solving and negotiation   103

4.1 Design and write a children's book	104
4.2 Dinosaur dilemma	108
4.3 Create a circuit	112
4.4 There's a chance	114
4.5 Represent an issue	116
4.6 Imagine a world	118
4.7 Workers' negotiation	120
Problem-solving and negotiation: Moving forward	122

Part three: Where to from here?   125

A gender inclusive curriculum   126

Developing your own gender inclusive activities	126
Generic key questions to explore gender dimensions	127
Planning gender inclusive units of work	128
Conclusion	132

Blackline masters   134

References and bibliography   144

Index   148

Preface

Gender Dimensions is based on the premise that assertive speaking, active listening, cooperative learning, negotiation and problem-solving are skills which all children need to learn and to practise in a variety of contexts.

Children's understandings and development of these skills will be influenced by the values and beliefs they bring to the classroom, including those concerning 'appropriate' masculine and feminine behaviors. Similarly, teachers bring their own prior experiences, understandings and beliefs into the classroom. In order to help children to develop these skills, teachers need to be aware of their own understandings about gender. Additionally, their own skills in assertive speaking, active listening, cooperative learning and negotiation will need to be developed.

To help teachers to clarify their own beliefs and practices, we have included, throughout the book, questions and reflections for teachers to consider, along with support material. The activities aim to promote observation, reflection and skill development which will contribute to more effective and ultimately more rewarding classroom teaching/learning. The activities are designed to integrate aspects of gender, curriculum content and skill development in a meaningful way.

The book supports teachers who wish to establish a constructive classroom where:

- the importance of gender is acknowledged
- boys and girls respect each other as friends
- all children are valued
- children learn the skills of working together
- responsibilities and classroom management problems are shared
- children develop sound communication and life skills required for effective participation in society

Acknowledgements

Material in this book has been trialled in classrooms. We would like to thank the following consultants, teachers and students for their assistance and feedback. Their comments, questions and willingness to share their ideas with us has been most valued.

>Carmela Bianco, Ruth Blair, Di Bretherton, Carol Driscoll, Debbie Ford, Pam Hoyne, Sheryl Page, David Stevens, Sue Purves, Lesley Wing Jan, Cherylene Borbely

Many of the ideas have evolved and developed from the framework used in the Afters: Gender and Conflict in After-school Care research project and the STAGES (Steps Towards Addressing Gender in Education Settings) research project. Thanks also to Sean Pigdon for his technical assistance and to Maxine Cooper.

PART 1

STARTING POINTS

Introduction to *Gender Dimensions*

Gender Dimensions outlines activities which may be used in the classroom to address gender equity through the curriculum. The activities aim to enable the teacher and students to establish a constructive learning environment and to develop positive interpersonal skills.

A **constructive learning environment** is one where, on a day-to-day basis, girls and boys learn and practise the skills to enable them to see each other as friends; skills which they will continue to need and use throughout their lives.

Over the last fifteen years, as teachers have taken up the issues of gender equity in the classroom, a range of ideas and strategies have been explored. Some research, for example, suggests that in teacher-centred classrooms, boys gain up to two-thirds of teachers' time and attention, while many girls receive less than their fair share and have unequal access to resources such as playground space, computers and other equipment (see for example, Spender & Sarah 1980; Sadker & Sadker 1982; Clark 1989). Additionally, unexamined assumptions about 'appropriate' behavior for girls (e.g. 'ladylike', cooperative, helpful, good) and 'appropriate' behavior for boys (e.g. active, interested, disruptive, competitive) may often serve to limit the ways girls and boys are encouraged to engage in a wide range of activities.

Access and equity

Using this research to address gender equity, teachers work to ensure that girls have **real** access to resources including teacher time, space in the classroom and in the playground, and to equipment such as balls, bats and computers. But teachers will recognise that simply making available the *opportunity* for sharing resources is not enough to genuinely challenge unfair practices, or to stop the demanding and selfish behavior of some students (often particular boys), which gains them a disproportionate share of classroom resources.

The group-building activities in Part Two aim to enable children to get to know and like each other and to see the importance of fair access to teacher time, equipment, attention and space for more equitable participation of everyone. At the end of each activity, there are a series of gender dimension questions to enable teachers to monitor and analyse the interactions between students.

Valuing women's and girls' interests and contributions

Other research in the area of gender equity has challenged the ways in which women's and girls' interests and skills are not adequately acknowledged or catered for in curriculum content and teaching strategies. This approach toward a more inclusive curriculum draws on the work of a number of educational researchers including, for example, Gilligan (1982; 1988), Harding (1984; 1985), and Adams & Walkerdine (1986).

These researchers argue that because of different experiences which many girls bring to the classroom, they often have also developed different skills, skills which are not always readily valued within existing classroom practices. A sound principle of good teaching is to 'start from where our students are at'. This means that we, as teachers, need to recognise the strengths that girls as well as boys have developed from their different experiences and to provide a curriculum which acknowledges the many and diverse contributions which women, as well as men, have made to our culture.

By altering what we teach to ensure that it is of interest to girls as well as boys, and presenting, in the content of the curriculum, women's contributions and lives as of equal interest, the curriculum itself can be changed to become more inclusive (Swartz, Allard & Matthews, 1989). The activities in Part Two aim to cater for a range of interests. Part Three offers guidelines for teachers to develop their own gender inclusive curriculum suitable for their own contexts.

Additionally, much research (e.g. Slavin 1985; Dalton 1985; Wilson & Egeberg 1990) suggests that the use of cooperative learning strategies provides a sound educational framework for students to learn and share new skills. This may be especially beneficial for some girls since the focus is on shared tasks to which everyone must contribute. Cooperative learning can shift the focus away from the disruptive students and ensure that the quieter, less confident students also have the chance to participate.

However, using cooperative learning strategies without attention to the gender relations within the group may not be enough (see for example, Wilson & Allard 1993). Unless the skills needed to perform in the group are taught, and everyone is expected to contribute, the more able or cooperative students (often girls) can end up doing most of the work. The communication and cooperative learning activities sections, particularly, aim to teach the skills and to suggest ways in which teachers and students can address the issues of equal contribution and fair participation. Through such activities we can build on and endorse girls' skills and enable them to feel pride in their own achievements.

Valuing differences

As teachers, we know that what works for some girls does not necessarily work for all girls; the same may be said for boys. Differences among groups of girls and among groups of boys also need to be recognised when addressing gender equity. Recent research has paid attention to the ways in which race, class and ethnicity inform students' understandings of gender (e.g. Weiler 1988; Jones 1989; Wyn 1990; Hlebowitsch & Tellez 1993). It is important that we as teachers understand how beliefs about gender, about 'appropriate' masculine or feminine behaviors intersect with understandings concerning race, ethnicity and class, for example. Such beliefs, which children bring to the classroom, are individually as well as culturally learned. If we are to actively engage with our students, we need to understand where our students are 'coming from'. Through the range of activities offered in Part Two, we can better inform ourselves about, and build on, the diversity and strengths which girls and boys bring to their interactions.

How girls make sense of the world need not be limited to only the 'socially approved' ways of demonstrating their femininity. Similarly, boys, because of the limited 'masculine' behaviors encouraged within our culture, are too often restricted in the ways they interact with each other, the ways in which they can express a range of emotions or in their ability to understand the dynamics and participate actively in groups.

By valuing differences among girls as well as among boys, by recognising the ways in which class, race and ethnicity influence gender understandings, teachers encourage students to explore and appreciate real diversity rather than limiting expectations. We need to take the time to listen to girls and to involve our students in setting learning goals which are meaningful to them individually as well as collectively. The skills of negotiation and problem-solving, highlighted in the activities section, aim to enable a range of voices and understandings to be acknowledged and reciprocated amongst all students.

Challenging and critically examining the social structures

Another body of research which explores gender equity issues offers insight into the ways in which girls and boys can take up a range of femininities and a range of masculinities (e.g. Davies 1989, 1993; Mac an Ghaill 1994). This research explores the multiplicity of gender understandings.

Connell (1987) offers a useful analysis of how social structures, including schooling, can work to reward and to privilege particular masculinities. Certain masculine behaviors are assumed (often without examination) to be 'normal' or 'natural' and are often accepted, or at least tolerated, as 'the norm'. Power over others is asserted through such practices including sex-based harassment. When such behaviors are ignored, trivialised, dismissed or tolerated by those in authority such as teachers, particular masculinities become seen as acceptable social practice.

Another way in which particular practices empower and privilege particular 'masculine' ways of knowing is through the curriculum (hidden and overt) including content, teaching and assessment practices. The hierarchical structure of schools also subtly legitimises the authoritarian power-over mode of management rather than more collaborative, democratic approaches.

Other research (e.g. Gilbert 1987; 1989) suggests that the system of language as it is used in the classroom, in textbooks and in resource materials can work to limit understandings of 'appropriate behaviors' for girls and for boys. A number of the activities in Part Two use language as a starting point to explore these beliefs and to enable children to see beyond the limitations of gender stereotyping.

The final aspect of moving toward a more gender inclusive and constructive learning environment requires that we, as teachers, begin to understand and challenge the ways such social structures and practices enforce particular masculine behaviors which can be detrimental to women and girls. The Background Information and Gender Dimension questions, included in each activity, aim to help teachers toward an understanding of these issues.

Clarifying the terms

We use the word 'sex' to refer to biological, reproductive characteristics; that is, we are born as male or female. However, gender beliefs about what is acceptable *feminine* or *masculine* behaviors within a particular culture are not inextricably linked to our biological sex but instead are learned in an ongoing way. Such beliefs are influenced by a person's ethnicity, by their social class, by their race as well as their age, for example. Such beliefs are changing and changeable. They are negotiated on both an individual and a collective basis (Allard, Cooper, Hildebrand & Wealands 1995).

Sequence of skill development

While the interpersonal skills promoted here (communication, cooperation, problem-solving and negotiation) can and should be practised in a wide variety of situations and across learning areas, it is important to follow the sequence of skill development as set out in Part Two. For example, students need to have some knowledge of how to listen actively and speak assertively in order to negotiate successfully. The model in Figure 1 (p. 8) presents this sequence and was developed and trialled in our work with teachers and students at tertiary and primary levels.

Not all activities will be appropriate for all classrooms. Teachers who know their students well will be able to choose the most appropriate for their particular group.

Teachers are also strongly encouraged to adapt the suggested activities, develop their own units of work and to revisit all the skill areas frequently while keeping a careful check on the gender dimensions of students' endeavors. The process of change is ongoing and multi-dimensional. Teachers will need to do some of their own classroom investigations and supplementary reading provided in the reference list.

Elements of a constructive learning environment

The classroom environment should encourage and support all children to learn to work together as friends and work together to learn. A constructive learning environment recognises the contributions, skills, knowledge and experiences of girls and boys. The elements of a constructive learning environment are:

- active involvement in group building
- effective communication
- cooperation: cooperative behavior and role-taking
- effective problem-solving and negotiation

Figure 1 shows how the skills related to these elements need to be built upon in order to create a constructive environment. Group building is seen as the essential building block or starting point: a cohesive team spirit needs to be built and maintained.

A constructive learning environment is established when

- group-building has taken place
- children use effective communication, and cooperative, problem solving and negotiation skills
- teachers are actively working towards addressing gender equity.

A constructive learning environment is an outcome of skill development, and is facilitated by teacher awareness and reflection.

We believe that group-building activities should be used regularly throughout the year to build and maintain trust and positive classroom relationships; a prerequisite for developing communication skills. Because effective communication skills are vital for all children, especially when they engage in cooperative learning, at least some

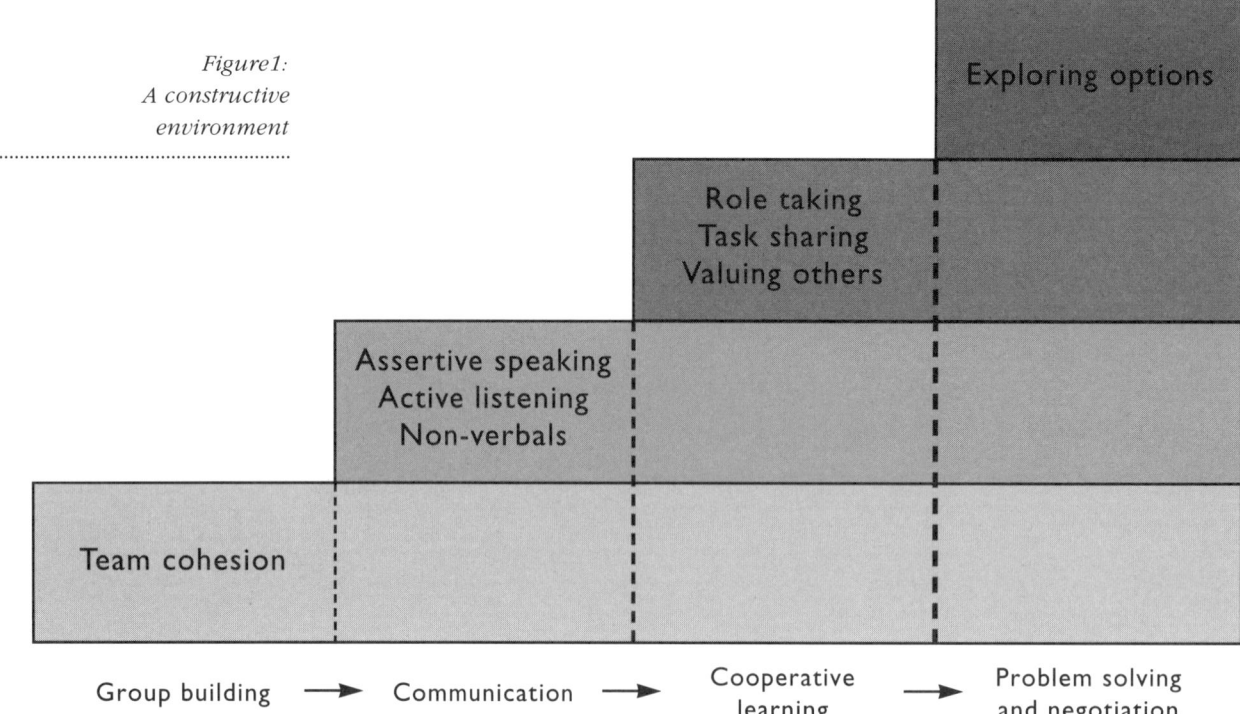

Figure 1: A constructive environment

communication activities should be used before using the cooperative learning activities in Part Two.

Successful problem solvers and negotiators depend on their communication and cooperative skills and experiences. Therefore, it is advisable to ensure that activities in these areas have been used first.

Although it is not necessary to use every activity in sequence, it is suggested that teachers select a sample of activities from each section, starting with group building. Use your knowledge of your children's skills when you choose activities.

Active involvement in group building

Active involvement by all children is promoted through group-building activities. Children are actively involved when they take responsibility for their own work and contribute to group efforts. When children are working together they share roles and cooperate to achieve the task. But the issue is a complex one because different groups of girls and boys may demonstrate active involvement in different ways. For example, children from different ethnic backgrounds may bring different understandings to team participation.

Some children may be actively involved in some activities but not in others, due to factors such as content knowledge, instructions, grouping strategies and other group members. Blackline Master 1 can be used to monitor and reflect on participation. Children can also be taught to monitor participation, helping them to develop awareness of fair play and equal participation.

Communication

Communication is enhanced by the understanding of non-verbals, by active listening and by assertive speaking.

Non-verbals

Non-verbal communication occurs when meaning is conveyed, often silently, through body language. Non-verbals are used as cues when trying to interpret how others are thinking and feeling and it is important for listeners to understand them. They can also be used by the listener to indicate to the speaker that they are being heard.

When there is an obvious distinction between what is being said and done, attention to non-verbal language can help to unravel the mixed messages being conveyed. All children need to be able to 'read' a range of non-verbal cues, which may differ according to the sex, cultural background and class of the speaker.

Active listening

Active listening is when children are able to 'hear' what others have to say. To achieve this, children (and adults) may need to put aside their own feelings and perspective on the topic of discussion while listening to others. Active listeners use strategies to ensure that they understand the speaker's message. It should be noted that while some girls may be quiet, they may also be actively listening. Children from different ethnic backgrounds may demonstrate their active listening in different ways.

Assertive speaking

Allard, Bretherton and Collins (1992, p. 12) define assertive speaking as: 'The ability to state clearly one's own thoughts and feelings without impinging on the rights of others.'

Elements of a constructive learning environment

An assertive speaker is able to honestly verbalise their needs. They do not blame others for the problem or impose upon other's needs. Assertion should not be confused with aggression. Aggressive statements impinge upon the rights and feelings of others. Assertive speakers expect to be heard but don't expect that they will always get what they want.

What do girls say about communication?

The following quotes were taken from an interview with three girls in year 4.

Interviewer: What does a good speaker do?
'A good speaker listens well, takes notes, speaks clearly and confidently. They read a lot, yeah, they take things in from books and remember those things and if they have to they can say "I've got the answer." When they speak they have idiot cards or a sheet of paper to read. They don't glue their nose to the paper though. They look up confidently. Sometimes the boys are the most confident but they also fool around. They think it is girls' stuff.'

Interviewer: What do good listeners do?
'Really good listening is when you understand quite well, you listen to other people and you also add to that. Maybe someone has a good idea, you might add on to it.'

'Sometimes you want to say something but there's just some people in our class, I can't name them 'cause I don't really want to hurt them but sometimes they don't let anyone else get a word in. That's it, it's not sorry or anything. It depends who is in your group, and [names two boys], they'd fight like mad. It is normally the boys but it is the girls sometimes.'

Interviewer: Have you heard of the term 'aggression'?
'Is it anger? hate? Where you discuss things and one person decides something ... where one person ends up winning and the other person gets deeply offended.'

Interviewer: Do you see it at school?
'Yeah, I see it a lot. You see it in the yard, kids are fighting. When they get angry, they can't control their anger, fighting, slapping. [names a particular boy], he's got a bit of a problem — it's not his fault. The other boys set him up, tease him. They like to see him get into trouble. But the teacher doesn't notice until one day. The boys tease him — he gets offended and punches and hits. But

sometimes he hits at someone who is very innocent, like the day he gave [names a girl] — she had a huge red mark on her arm and the teacher said if that had actually been him when he was a grown up, it would have been women abuse.'

What do boys say about communication?

Interviewer: What do you understand about communication?
'It's air mail.'

Interviewer: Does this happen in your class?
'Yes between the girls. They're always writing to each other.'

Interviewer: What do good listeners do?
'You have to concentrate, or you get blasted for not listening.'

Interviewer: What else?
'Look at people in the eyes. You have to be able to understand what they are on about or else you can't use it.'

Interviewer: What would you use it for?
'Homework and instructions. Then do what you're told but others [non-listeners] wouldn't hear what they've been told about what to do.'

Interviewer: What do good speakers do?
'Good speakers look at their audience. They speak clearly and loudly. Not look out the window and not look at their notes much. They don't write out the whole speech, just have key points.'

Cooperation

Cooperative behavior is when children work together to learn with and from each other. Children who cooperate with others have good communication skills. They recognise their own rights and those of others, they are able to assert their own opinions without fear of the ramifications and are willing to listen to the ideas of others. When working together they share roles, responsibilities, materials and the outcomes.

What do girls say about cooperative learning?

The following quotes were taken from an interview with four year 6 girls.

Elements of a constructive learning environment

'In group work, they [the boys] make you do all the work.'

'The boys say we're smarter than them. They always give us their work to correct.'

'They don't cooperate.'

'Yeah, they just sit there and say "Write this down" and "Start thinking" and they just sit there.'

'They never participate and they make funny noises in class ...'

'They just say "We're not going to do it." They just talk to each other and then turn around and say "Start thinking about things."'

'At the end they take the credit and say 'I thought of that.'

What do boys say about cooperative learning?

The following quotes were taken from an interview with three year 3/4 boys.

'Group work is good. You get to work with each other and get to know people more. It's easier to work with six than with one person.'

'You get more help. You get more done quicker ... but some kids might work faster.'

Interviewer: Are there some group members who don't pull their weight?

'Boys.'

Interviewer: Why?

'They might not try or they might not listen on the floor. They might not know what to do. They might not want to.'

Interviewer: Is it better to work with just boys or when boys and girls work together?

'Boys and girls work better together.'

Interviewer: Do you pull your weight in group work?

'Sometimes girls are bossy.'

Interviewer: Does that make you work harder?

'We get angry, cross and frustrated. We slow down and stop.'

Interviewer: What should be done so that you will do your share?

'They [the girls] should leave us alone. They can do their thing and we might help them. We could get a lot done if they just let the boys go for a while and they'll [the boys] get bored and then they might do the work ... maybe.'

> I like group work because. I think it would be more interesting with other Kids and if you get (stuc) stuk you can ask someone in yor group and if you ned a word you can ask someone and you co have company while you are doing it. you can make frinds, you can get it done qiker.

> * In my group there were [4] girls and [2] boys.
> * The girls did pay a tentrnon and listEn
> * The boys did Notting and Sat on muse chears
> * I like group work because you haf to work and you wright
> * The thing I don't like about group work is Mattew talks and Dussen listen

Problem-solving and negotiation

When children are required to solve problems together they draw upon their communication and cooperative skills. They need to reflect upon their understandings of the task and generate possible solutions and approaches. After listing a range of options (sometimes this is done through brainstorming) children can then begin to select and eliminate alternatives. Results need to be agreed upon, justified and communicated to others. Decision-making and negotiation are intrinsic to the process.

Elements of a constructive learning environment

Negotiation is a process that aims to give all parties a say in how a dilemma, a problem or a conflict can be resolved. Instead of one person always demanding and getting their own way, real negotiation allows everyone to contribute their own ideas, needs, concerns in order to come up with a resolution that is acceptable to everyone.

Negotiation often is mistaken for acquiescence. When one or two people insist that their ideas are the best, and refuse to actively listen to others and to consider other people's needs, this often results in others 'giving up' and 'giving in'. Giving in without being heard, giving up one's own ideas simply to maintain the peace or to reach any solution, is not real negotiation.

Beliefs about a constructive learning environment

A cooperative, constructive learning environment is established by teachers and children who:

- take the time to develop team cohesion and communication skills
- are willing to investigate cooperative learning strategies
- value difference and collective expertise
- know how to use and value active listening and assertive speaking
- see conflict as an opportunity to learn rather than something to be avoided (never accept put-downs or harassment)
- regularly assess group skills and set goals together
- use their power to ensure that others can use theirs
- reflect often on their own learning, group skills and understandings of gender
- monitor their own interactions with other people to ensure this is constructive
- make changes slowly, review regularly and recognise that mistakes are a part of learning
- acknowledge that change is difficult but worthwhile
- celebrate their own successes and support other teachers and children

Starting with ourselves: Teachers and change

Understanding ourselves

When considering how best to create a constructive environment for the children we teach, we need to consider how gender understandings influence the way we use language and the way we organise the classroom, as well as the content we teach. How do these beliefs influence our children's behaviors and skill development? Boys and girls, because of their different social experiences and different understandings about what is 'appropriate' masculine or feminine behaviors, will usually come to the classroom with different areas of expertise and we need to recognise how gender beliefs can limit students' development and to acknowledge their different starting points.

We need to take account of the diverse experiences and hidden assumptions that children bring to the classroom concerning gender 'appropriate' behaviors and, just as importantly, we need to become aware of our own understandings about gender. By examining these, we can develop a better insight into our own lives and how we might influence others, knowingly or unknowingly, through our actions based on these values. Often we may espouse particular beliefs about what we consider are acceptable behaviors for girls or for boys, without realising where and how we came to believe in them. By making them explicit, we can better consider whether they benefit or limit our own development as teachers, our interactions with children, and children's own understandings of 'appropriate' masculine and feminine behaviors.

What are your personal beliefs about 'appropriate' feminine behavior? Do you consider it appropriate for young women to be as ambitious in their career goals as young men? Do you believe that the traditional occupations of teaching and nursing are still the most appropriate choices for women? How responsible for looking after children should men be? Do you believe that their most significant contribution to the family still remains that of breadwinner? How do you interpret social constructions of masculine behavior implied by statements such as 'real men don't cry' and 'boys will be boys'?

Ethnicity and gender

An important influence on all of our understandings about gender appropriate behaviors is that of ethnicity. What ethnic background do you come from? How has your own background influenced your thinking about feminine and masculine behaviors? Are there certain jobs that are considered inappropriate for men from your cultural background? Are there other jobs that mainly women are expected to do? (Who cooks, cleans, mows the lawn, looks after the car, for example? How gender-based are these jobs in your own home? Why might this be so?)

Our students often come from a range of different cultures and bring with them into the classroom a different heritage, one based on values and beliefs that may not necessarily reflect or coincide with the dominant system of beliefs. By developing a greater awareness of, and sensitivity to, such differences in values and the behaviors which follow, we will be better able to engage with our students, to understand their lives and their goals. While we may not share the same beliefs, acknowledging the right to hold different values, sharing and celebrating difference, may be a necessary first step toward a classroom in which all children are treated, and treat each other, with mutual respect and concern.

Developing new skills: learning together

It is an important maxim that before we can teach others, we need to be learners ourselves. Sometimes we can learn alongside and from our students, not only by observing how they engage with new material, but also by noting the difficulties they encounter. This can help us develop our teaching skills as well. Many teachers will already be familiar with a number of the skills presented in Part Two. However, we have found from our own experience of working with students that we need to be familiar with and reasonably confident about using the skills ourselves before we can introduce them to others. We also need to be clear about how the skills interrelate, and why each skill is important in itself.

Group building

Group building may seem an obvious place to begin, but too often the pressures of time and the sense of 'urgency' about the overall curriculum, the material that has to be covered, can cause us to skip this necessary step in order to get into the 'real' work. An unexamined assumption which also creates problems is that putting children together in a class automatically makes them a group. This is simply not true. Time needs to be spent in helping all children become part of a coherent group.

Communication skills

Communication skills, particularly active listening and assertive speaking, do require practice. They are essential for children and adults if we are to work together successfully. Initially, if the children have not had much experience, the effort expended can be frustrating. However, if you have taken the time to explore and practise your own communication skills, you will be better able to see the small steps forward which children will make on a day-to-day basis.

Perhaps the best way for you to enhance your own skills in this area is to find a colleague with whom to practise and with whom you can share your attempts, frustrations and successes. Your reflections on these interactions can help you relate to the children's experiences.

Cooperative learning

Cooperative learning is where the outcomes of a specific task depend on all group members contributing to the group outcomes. Enabling children to develop cooperative learning skills and to work productively in groups presumes that you, as the teacher, have spent time investigating and developing your own understandings of, and skills in, cooperative learning. The 'Teacher Considerations' in each activity aim to highlight some of the values which underpin cooperative learning and to help you reflect on your own skill development.

Girls and boys practising active listening and assertive speaking in small groups

The activities are designed to help you prepare for and follow up the cooperative learning process. In order to be successful, they do require some preparation. However, again, once the skill development is underway, the time and effort required becomes less. It is worth persisting with the endeavors over a period of time; interspersing cooperative learning activities with independent work or with work in pairs offers to children a range of opportunities to develop different learning styles.

Problem-solving and negotiation

Problem-solving and negotiation skills also require skill development on the part of the teacher. Perhaps before beginning on this section, spend some time reflecting on your own ideas of power and negotiation. How important is it to you to feel in control in the classroom all the time? How do you feel about negotiating with children? How willing are you to allow them to have a real voice in the decisions that must be made in the classroom, including which rules everyone will abide by? Your personal values and experiences of power and how you see your role as teacher will affect your attitude to the role of negotiation. It is important to remember that negotiation is not the same as handing over all responsibility and power to the group. It does require, however, a real understanding of how you, as the teacher, choose to use your power.

Children negotiating roles for the problem-solving task.

How will you decide when children are ready to begin work on the skills of problem-solving and negotiation? By trying a number of activities in which you feel confident and reflecting on the children's processes of learning. What worked well? What needs more time and consideration? Involve children in this process of reviewing and reflecting.

Again, working closely with a colleague to practise your own problem-solving and negotiation skills will help to develop expertise and confidence when working with the children.

Teacher considerations

Throughout the activities, we have included a section called 'Teacher Considerations'. This often takes the form of a list of questions which aim to help you keep in mind some of the issues and concerns that might arise through doing the activities. Many of the questions focus on your own understandings and beliefs, encouraging you to make these explicit and so gain insight into how your values might inform your interactions with the children. The questions also aim to highlight how your children's understandings, not only of the skills but also their beliefs concerning gender 'appropriate' behaviors, might influence how they take up the new ideas.

Small steps toward change

Through the learning experiences we offer children, the ways in which they understand 'appropriate', often limiting gender behaviors, can be challenged, although developing new skills and understandings is a long-term, ongoing process. Rather than assuming that we can take great leaps forward to move beyond the often limited prescriptions of 'appropriate' behaviors, it is probably more realistic and productive to take a long-range point of view and accept that change will only come slowly!

The process is challenging, often frustrating, but in the long run also potentially rewarding. Keep in mind that small steps forward on a day-to-day basis is probably the most practical and realistic approach. Teachers, no matter how committed to change they are, still have limitations placed upon them by external factors such as time, the size of the group, difficulty in obtaining needed resources, demands of other commitments and the culture of the school they work in. Recognising these as real factors and working within such constraints can help to relieve the pressure and to keep setbacks from becoming overwhelming.

Remember, too, that any small step forward is worthy of celebration. The day that that difficult boy finally takes time to listen to another class member, the day that that silent girl offers to be the reporter for her group, should be acknowledged as significant change moments. Celebrate with your class and share your successes with a colleague. And finally, above all else, remember your sense of humor is probably your most valuable asset.

PART 2
ACTIVITIES

Learning area overview grid

Key learning areas	Studies of society and the environment	Science	Mathematics	Language	Health and physical education	Technology	The arts
Group building							
1.1 Terrific Terri name game					✓		
1.2 Fruit salad						✓	
1.3 Stomp						✓	
1.4 What do feelings look like?					✓		✓
1.5 Compliment bean bag					✓		
1.6 Jigsaw people							✓
1.7 Characteristics cube		✓					
Communication skills							
• *Non-verbals*							
2.1 What does listening look like?				✓			
2.2 Mirroring feelings							✓
2.3 Machine maker		✓					✓
• *Active listening*							
2.4 I feel ... when ...	✓			✓			
2.5 Representing feelings	✓						✓
2.6 Accident report				✓			
• *Assertive speaking*							
2.7 Blackboard target				✓			
2.8 Talk up triangle					✓		
2.9 Two-minute controversial responses	✓						
2.10 Take two							✓
Cooperative skills							
3.1 Build it together				✓		✓	
3.2 Paper Bag Princess: story map				✓			
3.3 Create a slogan				✓			
3.4 Collective cloze				✓			
3.5 Jumble and unjumble	✓			✓			
3.6 Body sculpture					✓		
3.7 Guess and check			✓				
3.8 Newspaper reconstruction	✓			✓			
Negotiation/Problem-solving skills							
4.1 Design/write a children's book				✓			
4.2 Dinosaur dilemma				✓			✓
4.3 Create a circuit		✓					
4.4 There's a chance				✓			
4.5 Imagine a world	✓	✓					
4.6 Worker's negotiation	✓						✓

Activity layout

The coding system specifies the year level that the activity is most suitable for. Most activities are adaptable for all year levels.

The main curriculum focus is specified. Sometimes more than one area is involved.

Learning purposes for each activity are listed.

This section discusses aspects of the activity which you may like to consider before use. It also raises some pertinent gender issues.

This section focuses on questions you might use to think about your own understandings and your communication and cooperative learning skills which can impinge upon children's learning.

Lists materials needed for the activity. Writing materials are not included as it is assumed these would always be readily available.

Number and title of activity

Suggestions for how to implement the activity are outlined in sequential order.

1.1 Terrific Terri name game

Level K–6
LANGUAGE

Purposes
- to help children to learn each other's names
- to help children feel positive about themselves
- to enhance listening skills
- to build team spirit
- to practise using adjectives

Background information

This activity can be used at the beginning of the year to ensure that children learn and use each other's names. It is also a useful short activity between sessions to reaffirm the sense of group.

Before using this activity for the first time, discuss with children how important it is for everyone to feel good about themselves. Girls in particular may feel uncomfortable about asserting their strengths since this often isn't viewed as 'appropriate' feminine behavior. Terrific Terri provides children with the opportunity to acknowledge and celebrate their own strengths, characteristics and abilities.

Teacher considerations

What are your strengths? Your 'best qualities'? If you were asked to describe your interests and skills to someone else, what would you say? Being able to say something positive about ourselves is often difficult. Yet if we can't honestly acknowledge our own strengths, how can we appreciate the contributions and talents of others?

Terrific Terri can provide you with an insight into how girls and boys describe themselves, what they see as important about themselves. For example, do girls choose adjectives that comment on their appearance more often than boys? Do boys emphasise their sporting prowess more often than girls? Should such differences exist?

What you will need

- Room to form a circle large enough to include all the children.

Each activity has at least two adaptations to cater for different needs. By adapting the activity slightly each activity could be used more than once to gauge improvement in skills.

This section poses gender equity questions for the teacher (and sometimes children) to consider after the activity. It is intended that these questions will raise issues of gender which you will consider for future planning and classroom change.

What to do

1 Sit with the children in a circle.
Explain that this is a language game where everyone needs to think of an adjective (describing word) that starts with the same letter of the alphabet as their own name. The word they choose must describe something positive or 'nice' about themselves. A few examples might be given such as Helpful Hamish, Friendly Farrah, Smiling Soula. Children should think of the word but not tell anyone yet.

2 Emphasise how important it is to listen carefully to how each person names themselves, since, as they go around the circle, each subsequent child must repeat the names and adjectives of all of those who have come before them before adding their own chosen description to their name.

3 If a child can't remember or gets stuck on one name, another child can mime the forgotten adjective to help the child to remember.

Gender dimensions

- Were there particular girls or boys who had trouble choosing a positive word to describe themselves?
- Who listened well? How was this acknowledged? By you? By the group?
- Were there some adjectives that only girls chose? (e.g. cooperative, kind, helpful, happy) Were there other, different ones that only boys chose? (e.g. mighty, strong, brave, clever)

Adaptations

- You could decide to do this in single-sex groups for the first time.
- Try playing the game without requiring the students to repeat all the names and adjectives that come before their turn: do they listen to each other as well in this situation? Have them choose a different adjective for themselves each time it is their turn.
- Record the adjectives as a written language activity.

Trialling comments

Year four boys found it much easier to choose a positive attribute about their comments. They were confident and sure about their comments. They cheered other boys when they said something positive about themselves. Most girls could not say anything good about themselves. They often used negative terms such as 'Dumb Denise'. Girls were embarrassed and sometimes physically removed themselves from the circle.

Observations and feedback are provided by teachers who trialled the activities.

Some reading ideas are included where they are relevant to activities.

Group building

Group-building activities are usually used at the beginning of a school year to develop class cohesion. Group-building activities are necessary to develop trust and to help every child feel a part of the class team. When groups work well together, it is usually because time has been spent helping members to get to know each other, developing trust and a sense of respect among members of the group.

Group building is seen as vital before children embark on mixed sex cooperative group work. Many interpersonal skills get in the way of effective cooperative group work. Lack of self-confidence, put-downs and embarrassment can inhibit the ways that individuals participate and gain skills from working together. For example, boys often ignore or personally criticise girls, many boys are not used to giving compliments and many girls are not used to receiving them, either from each other or from boys. Without a cohesive classroom, where children have learnt to accept and learn with each other, all children miss out in terms of their social and intellectual development.

Hill and Hill (1990, p. 12) explore the importance of gender issues in relation to team building:

> To create cohesion we need to look at the ways we inadvertently reinforce social structures ... The existing social groupings within any class are often accepted as a permanent reality. Boys choose to work with boys, girls work with other girls, the very articulate sit with other talkers and the quiet, withdrawn children sit alone.

Class cohesion established through group-building exercises is crucial for the development of communication, active listening, assertive speaking, problem-solving, negotiation and cooperative group skills.

The group-building activities that follow are generally straightforward and easily adapted to a range of different learning environments, from the first years of school to adult. The time spent in developing a group is, in the long term, well worth it. Children who learn to like and trust each other through shared laughter will be better able to work through difficult situations in a friendly manner and will be less willing to resort to aggressive behavior. Establishing a group to which everyone feels they belong will enhance participation and sharing.

Children engaging in group-building activities.

Group building

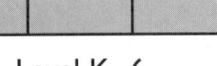

Level K–6

LANGUAGE

1.1 Terrific Terri name game

Purposes
- to help children to learn each other's names
- to help children feel positive about themselves
- to enhance listening skills
- to build team spirit
- to practise using adjectives

Background information

This activity can be used at the beginning of the year to ensure that children learn and use each other's names. It is also a useful short activity between sessions to reaffirm the sense of group.

Before using this activity for the first time, discuss with children how important it is for everyone to feel good about themselves. Girls in particular may feel uncomfortable about asserting their strengths since this often isn't viewed as 'appropriate' feminine behavior. Terrific Terri provides children with the opportunity to acknowledge and celebrate their own strengths, characteristics and abilities.

Teacher considerations

What are your strengths? Your 'best qualities'? If you were asked to describe your interests and skills to someone else, what would you say? Being able to say something positive about ourselves is often difficult. Yet if we can't honestly acknowledge our own strengths, how can we appreciate the contributions and talents of others?

Terrific Terri can provide you with an insight into how girls and boys describe themselves, what they see as important about themselves. For example, do girls choose adjectives that comment on their appearance more often than boys? Do boys emphasise their sporting prowess more often than girls? Should such differences exist?

What you will need

- Room to form a circle large enough to include all the children.

What to do

1 Sit with the children in a circle.

Explain that this is a language game where everyone needs to think of an adjective (describing word) that starts with the same letter of the alphabet as their own name. The word they choose must describe something positive or 'nice' about themselves. A few examples might be given such as Helpful Hamish, Friendly Farrah, Smiling Soula. Children should think of the word but not tell anyone yet.

2 Emphasise how important it is to listen carefully to how each person names themselves, since, as they go around the circle, each subsequent child must repeat the names and adjectives of all of those who have come before them before adding their own chosen description to their name.

3 If a child can't remember or gets stuck on one name, another child can mime the forgotten adjective to help the child to remember.

Gender dimensions

- Were there particular girls or boys who had trouble choosing a positive word to describe themselves?
- Who listened well? How was this acknowledged? By you? By the group?
- Were there some adjectives that only girls chose? (e.g. cooperative, kind, helpful, happy) Were there other, different ones that only boys chose? (e.g. mighty, strong, brave, clever)

Adaptations

- You could decide to do this in single-sex groups for the first time.
- Try playing the game without requiring the students to repeat all the names and adjectives that come before their turn: do they listen to each other as well in this situation? Have them choose a different adjective for themselves each time it is their turn.
- Record the adjectives as a written language activity.

Trialling comments

Year four boys found it much easier to choose a positive attribute about themselves than the girls. They were confident and sure about their comments. They cheered other boys when they said something positive about themselves. Most girls could not say anything good about themselves. They often used negative terms such as 'Dumb Denise'. Girls were embarrassed and sometimes physically removed themselves from the circle.

Group building

1.2 Fruit salad

Level K–4

PHYSICAL ACTIVITY

Purposes
- to build up group trust through shared laughter and movement
- to provide an opportunity for boys and girls to play together in a non-competitive manner
- to encourage children to share a limited amount of space

Background information

Because this activity does not depend on physical skills, it enables many girls and boys to participate without having to worry about being laughed at for making mistakes or about embarrassing themselves because they do not have prior skills. It also encourages the quieter students to get up and enjoy moving around rather than sitting quietly. At the same time, the game provides the opportunity for boys and girls to use space cooperatively.

Teacher considerations

When was the last time you joined a group of strangers? How comfortable are you meeting and mixing with people whom you don't know well? What helps you to feel more comfortable when meeting new people? Does it matter if the group you join is mainly male or mainly female? Do you have friends of both sexes? Reflecting on your own experiences and the skills which you have developed to meet new people may assist you to help children feel as if they belong and are members of the class.

Shyness or lack of social skills can be quite debilitating. Worry over what other people will think of you or concern about saying something silly causes some adults, as well as children, to remain silent. These real fears can make group participation quite difficult. On the other hand, some people are outgoing and very confident. It is worth considering: do you see girls who are shy and quiet as 'not a problem' whereas boys who are shy and quiet are of concern? Do you accept noisy and outgoing behavior from boys — but not from girls? Why? What are the gendered assumptions operating here?

What you will need

A circle of chairs with clear space in the middle of the circle and enough room for children to move. There should be one less chair in the circle than the number of participants, i.e. if there are 25 players, there should be 24 chairs.

What to do

1 Ask the children to sit in the circle of chairs.

2 Going around the circle, each child is given the name of one of three fruits, e.g. apple, pear, banana, apple, pear, banana, until everyone has a fruit name which they need to remember.

3 Start by standing in the centre of the circle and calling out the name of one fruit. Everyone who is that fruit (e.g. all the 'apples') must get up and quickly move to an empty chair, including the teacher. Those who are not 'apples' remain seated. Whoever ends up without a chair then takes a turn in the middle, calling out the name of one group of fruit again.

4 To get everyone to move all at once, the person in the middle calls out 'fruit salad'.

5 Once the children understand the game, speed up the time between children claiming chairs and the next person calling out.

Gender dimensions

- Did this activity encourage boys and girls to mix and mingle together or did they divide on the basis of sex?
- Was there pushing and shoving to get to the chairs? Who did this?
- Were some children left in the middle more often than others?
- Did individual children develop strategies to 'help' each other get to a chair?

Adaptations

- Vegetable names or names of colors are used. 'Mixed vegies' or 'rainbow' can be called out to get everyone to move at once. This can also be easily adapted to fit in with the current class topic.
- Non-competitive Musical Chairs
  Unlike traditional Musical Chairs, when the music stops, children who do not find a chair of their own can share one with someone else. Every time the music stops, another chair is removed. Eventually, only one chair is left and all the children must find a way to 'fit' onto the chair. This requires a great deal of cooperation and can be a lot of fun.

Group building

1.3 Stomp

Level 4–6

PHYSICAL ACTIVITY

Purposes
- to build up group trust through shared laughter and movement
- to provide an opportunity for boys and girls to play together in a non-competitive manner
- to encourage children to share a limited amount of space
- to develop eye–hand coordination in a fun way
- to develop/practise listening and direction-following skills

Background information

'Girl germs' and 'boy germs' are examples of insults used by some children to denigrate the opposite sex. Such insults keep children from playing together, and reinforce artificial boundaries that limit their chances to know and enjoy each other's company. Stomp is a game that depends on close contact in a non-competitive way.

Because few prior skills are needed for this game, those who have not played before need not fear failure or public embarrassment. This is also an interesting exercise in following directions since setting up the circle of hands initially can be a challenge.

Teacher considerations

How confident do you feel when you are asked to do something that you haven't done before? Do you feel anxious? uncomfortable? excited? enthusiastic?

The fear of making a mistake publicly and being laughed at for the mistake can create a reluctance, for adults and children, to join in new activities or take risks. Reflect on your own risk-taking skills and consider: What helps you to feel comfortable enough to take risks? What situations enhance your willingness to try something that you haven't done before? How important is sharing new experiences with others in the group? How do you react if you are laughed at? Why not share these situations with your class?

What you will need

Cleared space, preferably a carpeted area, large enough for all the children to get down on their hands and knees in a circle.

What to do

1 Ask everyone to get down on their hands and knees in a circle, heads facing into the circle. Your willingness to participate will encourage the more reticent children to do so as well.

When everyone is kneeling shoulder to shoulder, have each place both of their hands on the floor in front of them, with a small space between hands.

2 Then, each child lifts their right hand and passes it across the arm of the child on the right, placing it in between that child's hands. The two hands 'in front' of each child should now be the right and left hands of the child on either side.

3 When everyone has their hands in place, someone begins the game by 'stomping' once on the floor with their left hand. The 'stomp' is then continued by the person on their left's right hand, the person on their right's left hand, the first person's right hand and so on around the circle as if the 'stomp' is being passed from hand to hand.

4 When the children can stomp around the circle without pause, explain that to make it more complicated, anyone can stomp twice and this will reverse the direction of the game.

5 Speed up the stomps as the children become more adept at keeping the game going in both directions.

Gender dimensions

- Who listened well while the directions were given? How did you acknowledge this skill?
- Were there problems with children who did not want to kneel next to a child of the opposite sex?
- When mistakes were made, how did the children handle them? Did they see them as funny? Did particular children get angry? Were hurtful or ridiculing remarks made? If so by whom?

Trialling comments

It sounds complicated but actually it's very easy. I think a game like this is good for it gets the group close together and has no unequal emphasis on the one person, so everyone is involved and having fun. I think it's a good way to work on coordination with a fun game that has no competitive rivalry.

Level K–6

LANGUAGE/ DRAMA

1.4 What do feelings look like?

Purposes
- to build group trust
- to explore the importance of feelings
- to use mime as a way of conveying feelings

Background information

This is an introductory activity to help children begin to explore a range of feelings and to consider how these are conveyed through non-verbal communication.

Being able to recognise and to respect others' feelings is part of establishing trust within a group. Being able to 'read' people's feelings as they are expressed non-verbally is an important skill which will help children to develop greater sensitivity and insight into how they interact with each other. Different cultural backgrounds will also influence how children express their feelings non-verbally. This issue is also worth exploring with children.

Because of certain gendered expectations (e.g. 'big boys don't cry'), some boys are less able to talk about their feelings, and are less sensitive to how other people might be feeling. Because anger for many girls is directed inward rather than out onto others, they may have trouble expressing this feeling non-verbally. This activity can be used to encourage all children, particularly reticent boys or withdrawn girls, to value their own and others' feelings.

Teacher considerations

How sensitive are you to non-verbal communication? Can you tell when a colleague feels upset but says nothing? How do you respond to non-verbal clues? Do you think it is as appropriate for a man to cry as for a woman? For a boy as for a girl? How do you express happiness? How do the children let you know when they are feeling sad, happy, silly, etc?

What you will need

- slips of paper
- a bowl or a hat
- room for the group to sit in an open circle

What to do

1 Begin with a group brainstorm about feelings. On the board, write up the different feelings that children mention such as angry, pleased, sad, happy, silly, lonely, glad, etc.

Explain that sometimes we communicate how we are feeling through our actions or facial expressions rather than our words. This is called non-verbal communication.

2 Write the listed feelings on separate slips of paper. Have each member of the group pick one of these from a bowl. (Some might need to be repeated so that everyone has a turn.) Without telling anyone else what feeling s/he has drawn, each child is to think of how to mime this feeling. (How do they act when they feel this way? How do they stand? What do they do with their hands? How does their face show their feelings?)

3 Going around the circle, ask each child to act out that feeling without speaking. The rest of the group can guess what they are miming. When they get the correct answer, ask the children to explain how they 'knew' what the feeling was. What 'clues' are given to how someone feels through their facial expression, through the way they move, through their posture?

4 Discuss: Why is it important that we understand our own feelings? Why is it important that we are aware of how someone else is feeling?

Gender dimensions

- Which children were able to 'read' the non-verbal clues accurately?
- Were the same feelings mimed in different ways? Were these differences based on sex or different cultural backgrounds?
- What clues did children use to interpret feelings? Were these the same for boys and girls?
- Were there some children who found miming the feelings a difficult activity? Who were they? Why might this be the case?

Adaptations

- Have the children complete journal reflections about this activity. Some sentence starters examples:
    When I feel happy, I ...
    Feelings are important because ...
    If I did this again I would ...
- Monitor how children feel at various times of the day. What influences how they feel and how they express their feelings?

Group building

1.5 Compliment beanbag

Level K–6

PHYSICAL EDUCATION

Purposes
- to practise giving and receiving compliments
- to have fun and shared laughter together in a physical activity
- to practise throwing skills

Background information

Many children are not used to giving or receiving compliments. Girls, and some boys, often become embarrassed and recoil when compliments are given. Similarly, boys and some girls are more used to criticising each other than giving compliments. Often children who give compliments or applaud others are seen as 'sucks', 'mummy's boys' and given other less than complimentary names. When this happens, positive communication can be silenced.

It is worthwhile devoting time, especially at the beginning of the year, to making explicit ways of giving and receiving appropriate feedback, and to model and practise this regularly. It is vital that we reinforce the use of encouraging behavior and language. This activity is one quick example of how to do this. It can also be extended by using written follow-up activities.

Note: A beanbag rather than a ball has been chosen for this activity to avoid the possibility of criticism for poor ball handling skills.

Teacher considerations

When was the last time that someone complimented you on your work, your talents etc? How did the compliment make you feel? How do compliments concerning your appearance affect you? How well do you take compliments?

This game provides you and the children with a chance to compliment each other and, through this, to build up trust and acceptance within the group. There may be initial awkwardness in giving and receiving compliments but, like any other skill, children's ability will improve with practice. This game can be played on a regular basis and children can be encouraged to notice each other's positive qualities throughout the week.

What you will need

- one beanbag
- large space

What to do

1 Ask children to sit or stand in one large circle.

2 Start by throwing the beanbag to one child. At the same time they give that child a compliment about something they have done well. It may be related to their behavior or work.

3 The receiver then has to do the same. Rules can be made to enable everyone to have a go. For example: a boy must throw to a girl or a child with light colored hair must throw to a dark-haired person, or the beanbag must be thrown to someone who hasn't had a turn. The activity continues until everybody has had a turn or a time limit has been reached.

Gender dimensions

- Who were the children who found it hard to say something nice.
- Which children were able to accept compliments easily?
- How did they acknowledge the compliment?
- Were there occasions when boys made fun of girls? Vice versa? How was this commented on by you and by other members of the group?

Adaptations

- Use a ball when children have good ball handling skills.
- Make time for children to give each other and themselves a pat on the back.
- Put your 'warm fuzzies' in writing.
- Make a board with enough envelopes attached for all children. Post letters to each other giving compliments for things done well.

Trialling comment

When this activity was done in my K–2 multi-age classroom the children tended to focus on appearance. For example: 'handsome', 'nice hair', etc. Girls initiated compliments while boys tended to follow their lead.

Group building

1.6 Jigsaw people

Level K–4

ART

Purposes
- to use an art activity to develop self-confidence
- to allow children time to talk to and get to know each other
- to create a large display of class members
- to practise interviewing and reporting skills

Background information

It is crucial that children have a high level of confidence in themselves so that they are able to relate positively to their peers. One of the ways we can help children to develop their confidence is to give them time to talk about the things they are good at and proud of. It is also valuable for children to practise giving each other positive (instead of critical) feedback. These also need to be heard (see Communication: active listening activities).

While critical feedback about work may be constructive in some circumstances, personal criticism is very destructive to team building and self-confidence. Sometimes teachers ignore such comments to avoid confrontations or because they are seen as 'natural' for boys or girls of that age. We should not be complacent about this type of inappropriate behavior which can become aggressive, demoralising and ultimately seen by children as acceptable. If left unchallenged, this behavior can become harassment, even in primary schools.

Teacher considerations

How do you feel when a male/female family or staff member makes a derogatory comment about your appearance, your opinion, your competence? How do you handle the situation? Is it easier to ignore it or to comment assertively on your feelings concerning the comment?

How easy do you find standing up for yourself (and others) in situations where personal insults are passed off as 'humor'?

How much 'name calling' goes on between the girls and the boys? Do you see this as 'teasing'? Do the girls see it as 'teasing'?

What you will need

- large pieces of paper, thick felt pens and scissors
- paper bags or envelopes

What to do

To avoid the situation where some children might say they can't think of anything nice about their partner, before beginning the work in pairs conduct a whole group discussion about what could be written and then carefully select pairs.

1 Pair children up. Ask them to draw around each other so that each person has a silhouette.

2 Children then cut up their partner's silhouette into a number of pieces that you select. (The number of pieces will depend on the age of the children.) Pieces of each silhouette are placed in a paper bag, one per child.

3 Children interview each other and each writes something descriptive about their partner on each piece of their partner's silhouette.

4 When all pieces are completed, the pairs help each other to construct the finished silhouettes.

Gender dimensions

- Note the children who are able to give honest reports about each other. Who are the children who are having difficulties?
- Were all children actively participating in the task?
- Were the girls the ones who were sent to collect the materials?

Adaptations

- Complete this task over a series of sessions, slowly assembling the figures.
- Have several people contribute to the task of selecting the right compliment for the silhouette jigsaw.
- Make a display of all the bodies around the room and attach a complementary sign, for example, 'Ask us — we have a lot of talent in our grade.'

Group building

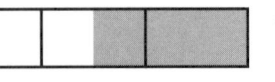

1.7 Characteristics cube

Level 3–6

MATHS

Purposes
- to encourage students to get to know each other better
- to promote self-confidence and team cohesion
- to emphasise that although everyone is different we often have shared interests, strengths and needs
- to develop students' mathematics skills of creating a 3D object

Background information

Children often do not have an opportunity to get to know each other's strengths, needs and interests. They can be reluctant to share these in case they are ridiculed. Children need to know that who they are, and what they are interested in, is viewed by others as important.

While this activity is based on groups of six, if children have not done a lot of group work together begin by using pairs or groups of three. Working in pairs before moving into larger groups can be less overwhelming for the quiet or less confident students. Dominant children can be given the task as a silent observer and the quieter children encouraged to be the speaker for the pair or group.

This activity begins with a whole class discussion, but if children are reluctant to speak up in the large group, conduct smaller share groups. After someone speaks, encourage others to compliment them on what they did well. Also, establish routines for monitoring who speaks to ensure that everybody gets a go. Children can participate in this process. By asking children to monitor your interactions with them, you are showing that you think the issue of everyone having a fair say is important to you.

Teacher considerations

Do you enjoy working in groups? Which groups? Under what conditions? What cooperative team skills do you have? How have you encouraged new staff members to participate in team work? Do the children have the opportunity to see how teachers also work as members of a team?

What you will need

- one square piece of cardboard for each person (e.g. 20 cm x 20 cm)
- drawing materials
- glue, adhesive tape and string

What to do

1 Conduct a class discussion about people's strengths, talents and interests. You may wish to start by sharing your own first. Be positive about your own abilities, as you are modelling appropriate behavior to your students.

2 Give students time to reflect on their own 'characteristics'.

3 First, ask each student to individually decorate a square piece of cardboard with their chosen characteristics.

4 In groups of six, children are to share their square and create a characteristics cube. Display these around the room.

Gender dimensions

- Did you ensure that all children had a say during the initial discussion?
- Were children able to accept what others had to say without sniggering, ridiculing and putting each other down during the class discussion and the group activity?
- Who were the children who actively contributed to making the cube? Who were the quiet children?
- How did the group resolve any differences of opinion?

Adaptations

- Individuals can create their own cubes. Each 'face' can display a different aspect of their interests and talents. Make time for children to share their finished products.
- This activity can be used to form groups; for example, all children who like animals could work together.
- Use the squares (or other shapes) for another maths activity such as tessellations or 3D shapes. Each child could be given one part of the whole to reconstruct.

Group building

Group building:
Moving forward

Now that you have tried a number of group-building activities it is an appropriate time to revisit and reflect on team spirit. This section helps to assist you to identify possible classroom relationship problems and their implications. Further teaching suggestions are listed to address your concerns and questions about interpersonal skill development. Some indicators of changed behavior are provided for diagnostic and evaluative purposes.

What is the problem?

- Some children:
    - don't actively participate in the process/task
    - don't do their share of group work
    - take over and dominate discussions
    - don't stay on task
    - refuse to participate.

- Divisions exist within the group.

- Particular children are being laughed at or ridiculed.

- Quieter boys and girls are being picked on.

- Girls and boys do not see each other as friends.

- Children are unwilling to trust each other and work together.

- Girls are being harassed.

What are the implications?

- Some children feel undervalued.

- Some children need to do more than a fair share.

- Some inappropriate behaviors are reinforced.

- Some children are silenced or ignored.

What can be done?

- Be explicit about the importance of working together.
- Praise children who show concern for others.
- Make time to discuss the importance of everybody getting a fair go.
- Model and implement a compulsory wait time after all questions.
- Give out talk tokens so that you and children can monitor who is speaking and who is not.

Talk token
This enables you to talk once during the session

BONUS Talk token
This enables you to talk 3 times during the session

- Ask the dominant student to be a silent observer.
- Put all dominant children together in a group and all quiet children in another group occasionally. Discuss what happened and how children felt.
- Consider alternative groupings such as single sex, friendship, interest and random.
- Choose some more group building activities which allow children to learn and use each others' names, where they share feelings, laughter and their commonalities.
- Some specific skill development may be necessary, for example: active listening or assertive speaking sessions.

> I liked this activity because we talked about feelings I was good at guessing One thing I didn't enjoy was doing the mimeing cos the boys fuss were whispering

Moving forward

Indications of changed behavior

- Everyone will do their fair share of the task.
- Each person will feel committed to the task.
- Children share credit for the outcomes.
- Everyone is showing responsibility for their own learning and the learning of others.
- Children know and use each others' names.
- Children are able to express their feelings.
- Children are able to work in mixed sex pairs/groups.
- Children show respect for each other, e.g. quieter girls and boys are listened to.
- Name calling, harassing and bullying behavior becomes less frequent.

> When I don't agree with someone I say I don't agree with you.
>
> When the grade works together when we get stuck they help me out.
>
> When we work in small groups we co-operate and help eachother

Where do we go from here?

- Continue to expand children's skills in taking responsibility for their own learning by having them make choices about their work and having them participate as a team member.
- Choose activities which challenge boys' and girls' understandings of gendered expectations.
- Discuss with children their feelings about friendship, participation and belonging.

Communication

This section is divided into three subsections: non-verbals, active listening and assertive speaking. In practice, these are interrelated. As you work through the activities it will become obvious how they are connected. They are separated in order to develop the specific skills and to make these explicit to the children.

What is non-verbal communication?

In the following activities, the term 'non-verbal communication' is used to include ways in which standing, walking, sitting, nodding, smiling, and other facial expressions, and hand gestures convey the way people are feeling without the use of words. Awareness of how we all communicate non-verbally helps children to understand the importance of 'reading' such cues as a way of interpreting what others are thinking and feeling.

Many girls are much better at reading non-verbal cues to other people's feelings than are many boys. This may be because 'appropriate' feminine behavior is thought to include the expectation that girls will be more sensitive, caring, nurturing simply because they are females. Yet such attributes are equally important for boys as well.

In order to develop sound interpersonal communication skills, all children need to be aware of their own feelings, of how their friends and other team members are feeling and to understand that feelings can be communicated non-verbally as well as verbally.

As active listeners, the use of non-verbal communication, sometimes referred to as 'body language', is a way for children to demonstrate to the speaker that s/he is being heard. Non-verbal indicators from listeners, such as nodding or making eye contact, are important in establishing communication, assuring the speaker that what they say is being listened to and considered.

When teachers make non-verbal communication skills explicit, discussing them and providing children with opportunities to practise them, those children who are unfamiliar with them can develop the skills. This also can assist speakers to talk about whether they felt they were being listened to. Indirectly, this works to enhance the classroom environment and builds the basis for effective cooperative team work, negotiation and problem solving.

It is important to note and to take account of the cultural differences in non-verbal communication skills. For example, while it is common within many Anglo-Celtic or Western cultures to assume that making eye contact is important, in other cultures (for example, among some Asian cultures) such non-verbal communication may be viewed as rude and unacceptable. These cultural 'norms' may also vary among groups of boys and groups of girls as well. Developing an awareness of cultural differences in non-verbal communication styles will work to enhance all children's communication skills. While differences need to be acknowledged in terms of starting points, a range of non-verbal listening skills also need to be taught so that all children, all girls and boys from all cultural groups, have the opportunity to know and practise different ways of responding.

Activities 2.1, 2.2 and 2.3 enable children to begin to explore non-verbal communication. These are starting points only and many other activities can be utilised to enhance children's understanding and awareness of this important aspect of communication.

What is active listening?

Active listening is much more than merely attending to what someone is saying; active listening is when the listener is engaged with the speaker and able to genuinely 'hear' what that person is saying — the feelings behind the words as well as the meaning and intention. Active listening is a difficult but extremely important skill to develop. If we actively listen to what someone else is saying, we feel as if we are putting ourselves 'in their shoes' in order to understand their ideas and feelings. Active listeners are able to suspend their own ideas and arguments concerning what the speaker is saying for long enough to enter into another person's point of view.

This does not mean that the listener gives up their own ideas and acquiesces to the speaker's ideas in the long run. In turn, active listeners have the right to expect that their ideas will be actively listened to as well. In terms of meaningful communication, sometimes suspending our own ideas long enough to genuinely 'hear' another person's ideas will enhance our individual ability to engage with those whose ideas are different from our own. This will create better opportunities to share differing points of view without needing to resort to talking over or insisting that our ideas are 'right'.

If children do not believe what they have to say will be actively listened to and valued, they are often silenced. Girls sometimes remain the quiet majority in the classroom if they think that what they have to say is unimportant or that they will not be called on and listened to when they put their hand up. It is therefore important that all children are heard and responded to fairly. Appropriate feedback demonstrates active listening.

'Polite' behavior is not necessarily the same as active listening. Sometimes the quiet students, because they do not distract others, are assumed to be listening when in fact they may simply be 'going through the motions.' This is one reason why it is important to ensure that the quieter children, often some of the girls, are given their fair share of time and attention and encouraged to demonstrate that they have, in fact, been listening. Listening skills need to be constantly recognised and acknowledged by the teacher and by other children.

If you have used Activity 2.1, it may be worthwhile to keep the brainstorm of suggestions concerning 'what does listening look like' up and to return to those behaviors as a reminder when children fail to demonstrate that they are listening. Part of active listening depends on providing non-verbal cues on the part of the listeners.

Activities 2.4, 2.5 and 2.6 aim to help children understand the importance of active listening and to build on their non-verbal communication skills as a way of demonstrating their involvement with what the speaker is saying.

What is assertive speaking?

Assertive speaking is 'The ability to state clearly one's own thoughts and feelings without impinging on the rights of others.' (Allard, Bretherton & Collins 1992)

An assertive speaker is able to honestly verbalise their needs. They do not blame others for the problem or impose upon other's needs.

Assertion should not be confused with aggression. Aggressive statements impinge upon the rights and feelings of others. Assertive speakers expect to be heard but don't expect that they will always get what they want.

Speaking assertively and listening actively are 'two sides of one coin'. Miscommunication can happen when the speaker asserts her/his own needs, concerns, ideas and the listeners are not actively listening. Alternatively, if the speaker is unable to assert her/his own needs, concerns, ideas, then this makes active listening very difficult. We end up feeling obliged to read between the lines — which often contributes to misunderstandings.

'I' statements are often used in assertive speaking. These begin with a simple statement of what the individual feels —'I feel anxious'; give a context for the statement — 'When I don't feel listened to ...'; and suggest a solution to the dilemma — '... and I would like you to pay attention to what I'm saying'. There are many possible variations but 'I' statements are important because they do allow the individual to express their personal perspectives, ideas, needs, concerns, or desires.

'I' statements are also often difficult to use because, for a variety of reasons, many children, as well as adults, do not believe they have the right to be heard. Alternatively, many children as well as adults are not used to actively listening to other people's ideas, concerns, feelings. Yet, if significant interpersonal communication is to take place, these reciprocal skills of assertive speaking and active listening are essential.

Children practise giving directions to each other outdoors.

Too often, we, as teachers, hope or assume these skills simply 'happen'. In fact, they need to be taught. And we need to acknowledge the gendered dimensions of such skills: in many cultures it is common for males to assert their ideas or needs and to expect that they will be actively listened to and attended to by females, and for females to be listeners rather than speakers or doers. No group in the long run, males or females, benefits from this limited and gendered bias in communication.

The best thing we can do is to provide all our students with the necessary skills, and to give them many opportunities to practise, to reflect and to respond to each other as people, as friends, and equals.

Assertive speaking activities, then, provide the means for girls and for boys to develop and to practise a life skill.

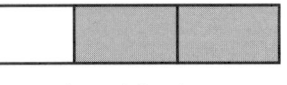

Level 2–6

LANGUAGE

2.1 What does listening look like?

Purposes
- to examine children's understanding of 'non-verbal listening skills' and to explore cultural differences
- to practise giving messages through non-verbal communication
- to explore how 'negative' non-verbal messages work against good communication
- to practise non-verbal listening skills

Background information

Some children have well-developed skills of paying attention to a speaker. Others are easily distracted, ignore the person speaking, make fun of the speaker or begin 'mini' conversations of their own. This activity aims to make explicit the importance of non-verbal listening skills such as eye contact with a speaker, sitting in an 'open' listening position, and giving cues to the speaker such as nodding, frowning, or smiling.

Some boys believe that what some girls have to say is less important than what other boys have to say and so when a girl begins to speak, these boys will often 'tune out.' This not only means that they fail to 'hear' what the speaker says, but also carries the 'hidden' suggestion that she doesn't have anything worthwhile to say. This is always disconcerting for a speaker and can be quite distracting for other listeners in a group situation. Such non-listening behavior frequently means that the teacher must intervene and call the distracted and distracting boys' attention back to the speaker, disrupting the flow of the communication and undermining the speaker's confidence.

This activity begins with a discussion on 'How do you know that you have been listened to?' which may be useful in drawing out differences in expectations and the range of good listening behaviors that are acceptable across different cultures.

Teacher considerations

How do you feel when you know you are not being listened to? What do you do? Some people become angry; others simply stop talking: what's the point, after all, if what you are saying is not 'getting through'?

How much time do you spend asking children to listen, to pay attention, to stop talking when someone else is speaking? This can feel repetitious and frustrating, and while it may seem necessary, teaching the children to monitor their own listening behaviors can be a more equitable and productive approach. The time you save can be better spent acknowledging and encouraging those listening behaviors that everyone needs to know.

What you will need

- butchers paper (optional)
- space for the children to sit in pairs
- a watch or clock for the timekeeper
- a list of topics on the board for the children to choose from (optional)

What to do

1 Begin with a group brainstorm on the topic, 'How do you know you have been listened to?' or 'What does listening look like?' Write the children's responses up on the board/butchers paper so everyone can refer to them.

2 On the basis of their responses, ask individual children to mime the different actions they have brainstormed. Point out how we can let the speaker know they are being listened to without 'saying' anything. Ask the children to explain what they understand by the terms 'non-verbal communication' or 'body language'. Help them clarify their ideas so that everyone has a clear understanding of the terms and how these relate to good listening skills.

3 Ask the children to pair up with someone whom they don't often work with. Encourage boys and girls to work together.

4 Each pair must decide who will speak first, who will be the first listener. The speaker must talk about a selected topic for three minutes. (They may choose their own, or from a range of topics on the blackboard e.g. 'My favorite sport is ... because ...' or 'The strangest animal I ever saw was ...')

5 Explain: the listener will use non-verbal language which demonstrates to the speaker that s/he is not listening. The speaker must attempt to capture the attention of the listener without resorting to physical contact.

6 A timekeeper (either the teacher or a child) tells the pairs when to start speaking/listening. (If a child does the timekeeping, this frees the teacher up to observe the different pairs.)

7 When one or two minutes are up, ask those who were speakers to describe the behaviors of the non-listeners. How did they know they weren't being listened to? (It may be worthwhile to write these up on butchers paper for later reference.)

8 Ask the speakers how they felt when they knew they were not being listened to.

9 Return to the pairs and reverse roles with the former speaker now becoming the 'listener'. This time, the listener must demonstrate through their behaviors that they are paying attention and involved in what the speaker has to say.

10 When time is up, ask a few of the speakers 'How do you know you were being listened to? How does it feel to be listened to?'

11 Discuss why these non-verbal listening skills are ones that need to be practised often.

Gender dimensions

- If there were boy–girl pairs, who was the speaker the first time? Was it more often a boy than a girl? Or vice versa?
- How did girls demonstrate 'non-listening behavior'? Were their behaviors similar to the 'non-listening' behaviors of boys? (less exaggerated? more 'polite'? etc.)
- If there are a range of children from different cultures in your class, were there differences among the children in how they demonstrated listening and non-listening behaviors?

  It may be worthwhile keeping the brainstormed suggestions concerning 'what does listening look like' on display and to return to those behaviors as a reminder when children fail to demonstrate that they are listening.

Adaptations

1 Divide the class into groups of three.

2 Ask each group to decide who will be the speaker, the listener and the observer.

3 Ask the speaker from each group to wait outside the room or in an area where they cannot hear the directions.

4 Distribute 'listener'/'non-listener' role tags randomly to the 'listeners' of each remaining pair. Explain that the observer in each group will keep detailed notes concerning the non-verbal listening/non-listening behaviors.

5 Bring the speakers back and ask them to begin their talk. Some of the speakers will be listened to; others (those in groups where the role tag specified 'non-listener') won't be.

6 Discuss how each speaker felt about their role.

7 Ask the observers to comment on the listener/non-listener roles. How did they convey whether they were listening or not?

There are many opportunities for observing non-verbal communication in the schoolyard.

Non-verbal communication

51

2.2 Mirroring feelings

Level K–6

DRAMA

Purposes
- to convey feelings about an event through mime
- to practise empathising with others' feelings
- to develop concentration skills
- to provide an activity for children to interpret non-verbal messages

Background information

Imagining how it 'feels' to be in someone else's position is one way of helping children to develop empathy with each other. In this activity, one child tries to mirror the responses/feelings of another to a situation. By physically mirroring the non-verbal actions which convey feelings, children can gain insight into how other people express their feelings through body language and facial expressions. They can 'try-on' a range of feelings. The observer, the third member of the group, attempts to work out what feelings were being conveyed in a particular situation and provides feedback to the pair on what worked well.

Teacher considerations

Considering how other people feel can be difficult for children and adults. It is vital to do this, though, if we are to become active listeners. Try reflecting on how well you do this with children and your peers. What non-verbal cues do you use to help you to interpret what the speaker is saying?

What you will need

- a range of situations written on pieces of paper, one for each group. You could use Blackline Master 5.
- a clear space for each group to work together

What to do

1 Allocate children into groups of three and ask them to decide who will be the 'actor', the 'mirror' and the 'observer'.

2 Explain that the actor in each group will be given a 'situation' to act out. They should keep this secret and think about how they can convey the situation and their feelings through actions only — no talking!

3 When each actor is ready, their partner will stand face to face with them and try to mirror their every action. The observer will watch carefully, try to work out what feelings are being conveyed and what the situation is all about.

4 When the action is finished, the observer and the mirror together try to guess the situation. When they get the right answer, they need to explain what actions helped them to determine what was going on. What feelings were conveyed by the movements of the actor? How accurately did the mirror respond? What difficulties did the person who was mirroring have in following the actor's movements? How did they feel?

Gender dimensions

- In the groups of three, who took the role of actor? In mixed groups, was it more often a girl than a boy or vice versa?
- Who, in the mirror role, concentrated well on the actions? How was this acknowledged within the group?
- How well did the observers provide positive feedback to the partners? Were girls more skilled than boys in this role?
- Did particular groups of boys or girls work well together? How was this acknowledged?

Adaptations

- Rotate the roles around in each group so that everyone has a chance at doing each one.
- Ask each group to demonstrate their situation for the whole class and let the class guess.

Non-verbal communication

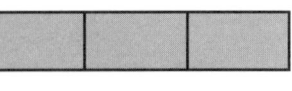

2.3 Machine maker

Level K–6

DRAMA/SCIENCE

Purposes
- to develop skills in non-verbal communication and movement
- to build team cooperation and enjoyment
- to encourage concentration and creativity
- to involve children in a cooperative drama activity

Background information

Often boys state that 'girls games are dumb', or 'girls can't play as rough as boys'. Many boys will play individually with girls but it isn't often that groups of girls and boys play publicly together. Yet, one means of establishing a friendlier environment based on mutual knowledge and respect is through shared experiences, especially positive ones. This game is an example of a simple but powerful way of helping girls and boys to work together to produce a shared experience. Such shared participation may help to establish and maintain friendships in and out of the classroom.

Some children may feel initial shyness at 'performing'. Building a machine in which they choose the motion and the sound they wish to perform encourages quieter children to participate since they can select a movement that they feel comfortable with. Different movements and sounds all work together to develop a whole machine; in this way, the importance of diversity can be recognised.

Teacher considerations

How much do you 'know' about machines? How adept are you at taking things apart and putting them back together? If you have had lots of experience in this area, you are probably comfortable with figuring out how things work. For other people, especially some women who have not had a lot of encouragement or experience in 'tinkering', machine parts can present a daunting challenge.

While this activity is based on building a 'fantasy' machine, the idea of working parts and 'assembling' the various parts can introduce children who have not had much experience of playing with machines to these ideas without provoking anxiety. In playing Machine Maker your own sense of creativity and fun are important. Your enjoyment of the game can work to encourage the children to respond positively as well.

What you will need

- a large cleared space for children to move freely in

What to do

1 Begin by discussing with the children the various machines that they use in their everyday lives. Encourage them to go beyond the obvious ones (e.g. cars, electrical tools, sewing machines) and to consider their own definitions of 'what is a machine?'

2 Explain to the children that they will be asked to create one machine which has many moving parts. Each of the parts makes one sound and links into at least one other part. Brainstorm as many different sounds as possible and consider how the same sound can be made different by using different rhythms (e.g. choo/choo/choo or choo-choo-choo/choo-choo-choo/choo-choo-choo).

3 Ask each child to choose a sound for the part they will become.

4 Form a large circle with the children. Explain that along with their sound, each part of the machine makes a different movement. Suggest and/or ask the children to demonstrate a wide range of possible movements. Then ask each child to choose a movement that they feel comfortable with and combine it with their sound.

Go around the circle and have each child demonstrate their sound and movement.

5 Tell the children that you are the Machine Maker. You as the Machine Maker will put the various 'parts' together and those parts must perform their individual movements and sounds as soon as they are linked to another part. They will need to continue doing their machine part while the rest of the 'machine' is being built.

Note: If the group of children is large and noise is an 'issue', it may be better to create the machine first with the children doing only their movements. Then, when everyone is in place and moving, tell them that you are now going to turn up the sound. As you move an imaginary dial to high, their sounds will increase, when you turn the dial to low, their sounds will decrease. Therefore, they must pay attention to how you turn the dial. When you turn the sound dial off, the noise should cease completely and quickly.

Non-verbal communication

6 Take photographs when the machine is completed, with all children involved in performing their 'part'. Alternatively, if videoing is possible, this provides not only the visuals of the machine, but also the sounds that the machine makes. These visuals can then be used to show the children how they looked when they were all working together and to celebrate the fantasy machine.

7 Discuss with the children: How easy/hard was it to come up with a movement and sound that was different from everyone else's? How easy/hard was it to concentrate on doing their 'part' with so many other sounds and movements around them? How did each feel about being part of the fantasy machine?

Gender dimensions

- Were some children more reticent than others to 'perform'? Who were they? How were they encouraged to become part of the machine? Who encouraged them?
- How well did particular children concentrate on their own movements and sounds? Whose attention wandered? Who did/didn't pay attention to the 'sound dial'?
- Was this activity of more interest to particular groups of boys? of girls? What did those who were less interested say about the activity?

Children creating parts to form their machine.

Adaptations

- Have children take turns being the Machine Maker.
- The moving parts of real machines can be used as a basis for this activity, e.g. in small groups, children choose a familiar machine such as an electric toothbrush or a camera and try to work out the various parts needed to make it operate. They then mime the parts and the rest of the group tries to guess what machine they are performing. Their ideas about what parts are needed can then be compared with actual parts of a camera etc. (See *Getting Into Gear*, McClintock Collective 1988, for an elaboration of this activity.)

Trialling comments

'During the initial discussion only boys had ideas about machines. Girls needed time to think about examples, then they had good ideas. Some boys took over groups. This depended on team members. Some girls organised groups. Some of the younger children were better at copying other children's actions.'

2.4 I feel ... when ...

Level 3–6

**LANGUAGE/
SOCIAL
EDUCATION**

Purposes
- to introduce active listening
- to encourage children to develop empathy for others
- to help all children to speak about their feelings

Background information

Active listening, as a skill, depends first of all, on a willingness to 'hear', an openness on the part of the listener to what the speaker is saying. The following activity concentrates on hearing, and sharing in, the feelings of the speaker. By way of introducing active listening, the topic under discussion is that of feelings.

However, as children learn and become more adept with practising the skill of active listening, they will become sensitive to the feelings of the speaker, even if these feelings are not made explicit. A sense of empathy will be brought to the listening situation, regardless of the topic under consideration. However, much practice is required before active listening becomes part of the repertoire of skills children use comfortably. Therefore, they will need many opportunities to practise active listening and the importance of this will need to be made explicit.

Teacher considerations

When you are listening to a friend speak, how engaged are you in what your friend is saying? How well do you actively listen, suspending your own judgement or comments in order to enter into their perspective?

Are you able to actively listen to colleagues and supervisors? How do you know when you are actively listening? How will children know when they are practising this skill?

What you will need

- butchers paper for brainstorm (optional)
- space for children to work in pairs

What to do

1 Begin with a group brainstorm about feelings. On the board, write up the different feelings that children mention such as angry, pleased, sad, happy, silly, lonely, glad, etc. (Or if you have done Activity 1.4, use the list brainstormed from that activity.)

2 Ask the children to break into pairs. One child will choose one feeling and describe a time when they felt that way to their partner. The partner must listen closely to what the first child says. They may ask questions if they want more information, but the important thing is to listen well because they will need to explain this to the whole group on behalf of their partner. When the first child has finished, they change roles and the second child speaks while the first listens.

3 Bring the group back together again. Explain that each partner will tell the group about their partner's experience of a particular feeling. When each pair is finished telling the whole group about each other's 'feeling', ask each member if they would like to add anything. Ask: Do you feel as if your partner listened to what you said?

4 When the whole group has listened to each pair, discuss: How many different feelings were shared? Why are feelings so important? Are there certain events that make us feel certain ways?

5 Explain that they have now begun the process of active listening. Explore with the children what this means in terms of the speaker, the listener and the ideas/feelings conveyed.

Gender dimensions

- If children chose their own pair partner, how many boy–girl pairs were there? (If children never choose to work in mixed sex pairs, how can you encourage them to do so?)
- Which children were able to accurately convey their partner's feeling? (Were these more often girls?)
- How well did the more dominant, demanding students listen to their partner? What did their partner have to say about whether they felt listened to?

Adaptations

- Change the topic to be shared. Other topics might include: 'The thing I hate most ...', 'My favorite place is ...', 'The person I would most like to be like is ...'.
- Rotate partners so that every time children do an active listening activity, they work with someone different.

2.5 Representing feelings

Level K–4

ART/SOCIAL EDUCATION

Purposes
- to explore feelings through visual representation
- to create an opportunity for children in mixed groups to discuss feelings
- to practise active listening skills

Background information

This activity asks children to work together to create a group collage representing how the group feels about a particular emotion, for example: anger or fear. They must listen to each other so that they understand other's feelings. This activity involves buddying so that each person is also an advocate for their partner.

Using a buddy system is a way of ensuring that buddies understand each other's feelings and that these can be restated. However, it does not guarantee that this will be the case. Boys and girls often need practice doing this. They have to know that this is an expectation. You will need to intervene with groups to help monitor interactions and keep check on put-downs. Ask questions about how buddies are helping each other. Give positive feedback to children who can convey their buddy's and their own feelings.

Teacher considerations

How important do you think it is for boys to listen to girls and vice versa? When you speak (for example at staff meetings) do you feel that you have been listened to? Are your feelings as well as your ideas considered? In what situations do you feel silenced? In what situations do your children feel unable to express their feelings? Have you considered why?

What you will need

- large pieces of paper
- thick texta pens, scissors and glue
- magazines

What to do

1 Brainstorm a list of feelings with the class. (Or use the list from Activity 1.4.)

2 Explain and organise a buddy system where a boy is paired with a girl. Discuss why it is important for girls and boys to listen to each other. Try random pairing where a boy and girl born in the same month are paired, for example. Explain the buddy system where each buddy listens and ensures that their partner's ideas are listened to by others in the group.

3 Group children into fours (two buddy groups).

4 Select one of the emotions on the brainstorm list for each group of four to represent as a collage using magazine cut-outs.

5 Remind children that everybody has a say in what pictures are selected for the collage. The final product must be a fair representation of the feelings of all group members. Therefore, before they start, the buddies are to listen to how they feel about the feeling to be represented.

Gender dimensions

- Were all voices heard and represented in some way on the collage?
- How did children work as buddies? Were girls more supportive of their buddy than boys?
- How well did the children listen to each other?
- Which children were unable to verbalise their feelings?

Adaptations

- Instead of brainstorming, write emotions on cards and give these to children to represent.
- Ask children to do the activity individually and then share the most appropriate magazine cut-outs to create the collage.
- Ask children how the activity worked. For example, pose questions such as: What did you like about the activity? What didn't you enjoy? How did the activity make you feel? If you were the teacher what would you change about the activity?
- Use Blackline Master 6 to assess children's feelings toward the task and to have them self-assess their own performance.

Active listening

Level 3–6

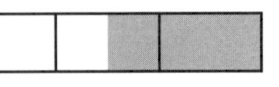

2.6 Accident report

LANGUAGE

Purposes
- to practise giving clear reports
- to consider the role of the listener and speaker in communicating an accurate message
- to practise active listening

Background information

This activity emphasises the importance of working together, setting aside personal differences and cooperating for a successful outcome.

In many situations it is crucial that messages be conveyed accurately and that the people involved understand exactly what is meant. This activity reinforces these points by asking children to restate accounts of accident reports. The activity assumes the children are familiar with role-play. If the children have not done this before, you will need to explain the process.

This task ensures that everybody has a job to pass on the message for the survival of the car accident victim. Some children (often the more competitive boys) blame other team members if the team fails to achieve their goal. This task encourages the cooperation and accountability of each team member. When children do not work well together they will not complete this task well.

When reflecting on the activity, ask children to consider and assess their own team participation. Initially, they may overestimate their own performance but generally they do not. Children are more likely to underestimate their work (especially girls). Individual and small group conferences can be held to monitor and encourage an honest evaluation.

Teacher considerations

When considering your own skills, how clearly do you give directions? How well do you listen to others when they are directing you? What distractions do you find 'irresistible'? In what situations do you find listening easy? What makes listening to others difficult for you? What kind of distractions might operate in your classroom? How do you deal with them for the benefit of the entire class?

What you will need

- space to role play

What to do

1 Ask groups of five to choose one role each from these: accident victim (car passenger), car driver, pedestrian, police officer and ambulance driver.

2 Ask the children to role play a car accident. The passenger is injured and must get to hospital as soon as possible. It is the responsibility of the car driver to tell this to the pedestrian who notifies the police officer who, in turn, contacts the ambulance officer.

3 After each person has played their part, they can no longer intervene in the communications.

4 Discuss the results of the role-play. How well did the characters listen to each other? If there were problems in communicating, was this because the character's account was garbled or did the listener not pay close attention? What could be done to improve the listening and the verbal accounts?

Gender dimensions

- How were roles chosen/allocated?
- Were roles stereotyped? (e.g. Was the car driver always a boy, the passenger always a girl?)
- How clearly did children convey their messages?
- Who were the children who did not listen well and were unable to pass on an accurate message?

Adaptations

- Perform this role-play in groups of six where one person is an observer. Have the observer take notes on the skills of the speakers and listeners. This requires clear criteria for the observer.
- Vary the scenario.
- Allow children to ask questions of others or help others out if they think the message is not accurate enough.

Active listening

2.7 Blackboard target

Level 3–6

MATHS

Purposes
- to develop spatial relation skills
- to practise speaking clearly and giving clear directions
- to practise working cooperatively

Background information

Giving directions is an example of how important it is to speak clearly. While giving directions is not the same as assertive speaking, it is a useful way to help children consider the importance of being clear about what they wish to say, and of thinking before they speak. Of course, regardless of how clear the directions are, if they are not 'heard' by the listener, nothing is accomplished. Giving accurate instructions and listening carefully take practice. Allow children to ask questions and have a go at restating what they have heard.

In this activity, children quickly see that they need to work with each other to reach the target. The audience, as well as the blindfolded person, needs to listen very carefully. If children criticise each other's directions or indulge in put-downs during this activity, it is worth stopping and reconsidering the importance of providing positive and supportive statements.

Teacher considerations

How do you feel when you are asked to do something new in front of a group? Do you feel anxious, excited, frustrated, nervous? When you feel this way, how easy is it to 'hear' what others are saying? How do you manage to work through your own feelings while achieving the set task? It is worth thinking of your own strategies in order to help girls and boys to discuss their experiences of speaking and listening within a group.

What you will need
- a large working space on the blackboard
- chalk
- blindfold

What to do

1 Explain to the children that this activity involves giving clear directions and listening well.

2 Select one child to be blindfolded. This child will be the 'drawer'.

3 Draw a cross on the blackboard within the reach of the 'drawer'.

4 Ask for volunteers from the rest of the class to give the blindfolded child directions to help them reach the target. No further instructions are allowed once the blindfolded child has started drawing. When the 'drawer' stops, another class member can give another instruction.

5 The game continues until the drawer puts a line through the target.

Gender dimensions

- What did children say that was encouraging?
- Were there some children who made fun of the blindfolded person's attempts? Did some children become angry or frustrated with the actions of the drawer? Who were they?
- Who were the children who were able to give clear directions?
- How well did the children listen to each other's directions?

Adaptations

- Make this more difficult by putting restriction on the number of instructions given.
- Play this game in pairs or small groups.

Assertive speaking

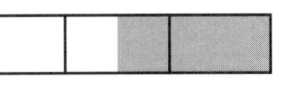

2.8 Talk-up triangle

Level 3–6

LANGUAGE

Purposes
- to practise stating one's own needs
- to actively involve children in considering the difference between assertion, aggression and submission
- to develop confidence in speaking assertively
- to discuss conflict resolution strategies

Background information

Some children are very good at conveying their opinions but they may do so aggressively. Other children, particularly some girls, may become quiet and withdrawn in conflict situations, surrendering their rights to speak and to be heard for fear of the consequences. Being able to state one's own needs and feelings without impinging on the rights of others is an important skill for everyone to develop.

It is valuable to note children who confidently speak up for their own rights and the children who continually act submissively or aggressively. It is also crucial that children themselves realise that they are responding to conflict in these ways. They should understand that there are a range of ways to behave and that, in different situations, some are more appropriate than others. During this activity children are asked to consider a range of ways of responding to possible conflict scenarios. They should be encouraged to consider all responses. You can use this activity as a springboard for more work on conflict resolution.

Teacher considerations

How familiar are you personally with the use of 'I' statements? Have you had the chance to practise and to use these in your own situation? Do you feel comfortable using 'I' statements or do you find them awkward or artificial?

Often, if we have not used them before, such statements may seem overly formal or constructed. Yet, 'owning' our needs and concerns can be an empowering experience. Remember, the use of 'I' statements does not automatically assume that we will get our own way; 'I' statements allow us to express ourselves assertively in a non-threatening manner, so that our listeners have the chance to know and to hear what we are concerned about. They enhance interpersonal communication because they are honest and open declarations. They do not rely on the listener to 'guess what I want or need'.

Again, assertive speaking using 'I' statements is a skill which requires practice. If you have not had much experience in assertively speaking, give yourself time and opportunity to develop this skill to ensure that you feel confident when you introduce it to your students.

What you will need

- three signs indicating the range of possible responses: assertive, submissive and aggressive. (These can be pictures or words.)
- the talk-up triangle scenarios (Blackline Master 7)
- a toy microphone (optional)
- a piece of chalk or string (optional)

What to do

1 Discuss with the children their understandings of the terms *assertion*, *submission* and *aggression* (see definitions p. 69). Explore with them the differences in meaning between the words. Pictures representing those ideas, for example, a shark for aggression, an ostrich for submission and an owl for assertion may be used. Place the signs on the floor in the shape of a triangle large enough for all children to stand within. Lines between these could be marked with chalk or string but this is not necessary.

2 Explain that the task is for children to consider what they would do given the scenarios. They need to decide where to stand on the triangle in relation to the marked points. Tell them that they should not just go where their friends go, and that they may be asked to explain their position.

3 Read out one scenario at a time. Children must physically place themselves near one of the signs according to how they would react. For example, would they react submissively, assertively or aggressively if kids have been tormenting them outside the toilets?

4 Using your toy microphone, ask a few children to explain why they chose to stand in that position on the triangle. Remind children that they do not have to justify their position; they can clarify it so the rest of the group can listen and understand. Consider the range of positions.

Assertive speaking

> **Where do you stand?**
>
> Color the spot which shows your reaction to the sentences.
>
> A=assertive
> Ag=aggressive
> S=submissive
>
> 1. You are the only girl in the group. The boys start telling rude jokes and you are embarrassed. What do you do?
>
> Comments: *Tell them to Shut up* 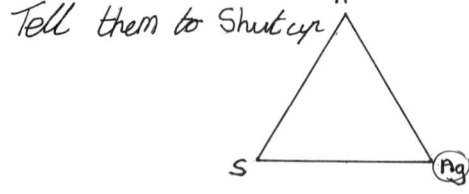
>
> (triangle with A at top, S bottom-left, Ag bottom-right circled)
>
> 2. Kids have been tormenting you outside the toilets. How do you react?
>
> Comments: *Pull a tantrum.*
>
> (triangle with A at top, S bottom-left, Ag bottom-right circled)

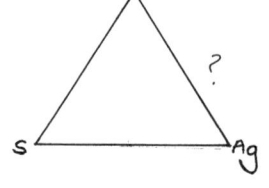

5 Generating a range of ways to 'handle' the situation can help children to understand the choices they have. The discussion is as important as the activity.

Gender dimensions

- Were there children who consistently placed themselves in the aggressive position?
- Did the girls often stand in the submissive position?
- Which scenarios were children able to respond to assertively?
- Were children able to 'hear' when others explained their positions?
- Which children were able to explain their choice clearly and confidently?

Adaptations

- Allow children to adjust their position after they hear someone else's opinion.
- Use statements to construct a scenario continuum worksheet.
- Ask children to generate scenarios to use in the triangle. Brainstorm different ways of responding to the scenarios.
- Use scenarios for role-play.

- Write your own scenarios to tie in closely to social or personal development or science and environmental education topics.

Definitions

Assertion is the ability to clearly state one's own thoughts and feelings without impinging on the rights of others. Assertive statements often begin with 'I'. They are honest, direct statements about how the individual feels, what they see their needs to be. Assertive statements do not lay blame on the other person or demand that the other person give up their needs. Assertive statements work to clarify how each person may see the same situation from their own perspective.

Aggression is often misinterpreted as assertion. However, aggressive statements violate the legitimate rights of others and are the insistence on expressing one's own thoughts and feelings regardless of the feelings or rights of others. Not listening to other people's feelings or needs is another form of aggressive behavior. Aggression is not a biological inevitability, i.e. not related to a person's sex, but a way of responding which the person many choose not to use.

Submission is the inability to express one's thoughts and feelings through fear of aggression or intimidation. This aggression or intimidation may not be explicit, but the underlying fear of it can work to silence individuals. They then give in to others' demands or wishes without ever clarifying or expressing their own needs. One's own rights are violated when one behaves submissively. (Allard, Bretherton & Collins 1992, pp.12–13).

Level K–6

SOCIAL EDUCATION

2.9 Two-minute controversial responses

Purposes
- to challenge children to present an argument
- to develop confidence in speaking to the class
- to provide an opportunity for children to listen for two minutes to the opinion of others without interrupting

Background information

All children need to develop the necessary skills and experience to speak confidently and assertively to large groups. This activity provides a situation where children have the right to have their say and be listened to.

Some girls say they do not like to speak before large groups because they are afraid of being 'picked on'. Quieter boys also experience verbal bullying when they try to make their ideas known to the group. To develop confidence in their own ideas and in their ability to present their ideas, all children need to have positive speaking and listening experiences. The chance to practise such skills in a supportive environment is essential. In order for everyone to benefit from the experience it may be worthwhile establishing clear guidelines for listeners. What is appropriate and supportive behavior? (It may be necessary to revisit some of the previous activities on group building and active listening if difficulties occur.)

If children are to give feedback to speakers publicly, provide parameters for this to ensure that it doesn't turn into a chance to 'have a go' at children personally. One way of doing this is to draw up an agreed list of criteria for giving feedback to speakers. Always monitor and acknowledge appropriate ways of responding to others.

Some suggested topic statements are provided on Blackline Master 8. It is important to point out to children that these statements, especially those about gender issues, do not represent facts. We wish to challenge rather than reinforce stereotypes.

Teacher considerations

Are you a confident public speaker? What do you like/dislike about speaking in front of your peers? It is worth reflecting on the factors that have inhibited or enhanced your confidence in speaking to large audiences.

Who are the most outspoken people at your school? Are they mainly men? When some staff (often women) don't have an equal say in contributing to the decision-making processes through discussion, the decisions may not be inclusive of everyone's needs or ideas. Sometimes it is useful to rehearse what you will say before important decision-making meetings.

What you will need

- a copy of Blackline Master 8 to distribute, or your own statements

What to do

1 Give each child or group a statement to consider.

2 Allow time for children to form their argument to present to others.

3 Remind children about the rights of others to speak without interruptions.

4 Conduct the two-minute talks in small groups or before the whole class.

5 Give feedback after the presentations either privately or as a group.

Gender dimensions

- How confidently did particular girls and boys speak?
- Were girls and boys able to listen attentively to each other without interrupting and/or making fun of the speakers?
- Which children need more practice in speaking publicly? Which children need more practice in listening well?
- How can different starting points be catered for?

Adaptations

- Have a jar of controversial statements ready to be used at times when you have a few minutes to spare.
- With practice children could speak without preparation time.
- Create statements that link to the classroom topic or gender issues.
- Ask children to create statements for talks.
- Shorten or lengthen the time of presentations.
- Prepare a list of criteria for assessing the speakers. Give feedback after the presentations.

Assertive speaking

2.10 Take two

Level K–6

DRAMA

Purposes
- to consider a range of ways of responding in conflict situations
- to practise assertive speaking through dramatic play
- to provide practice in active listening

Background information

Often, because of expectations concerning gendered behaviors, many boys' first response to a conflict situation is to act aggressively; many girls will seek to avoid conflict. These types of actions rarely solve the problem and sometimes amplify it. By considering and practising the different types of possible interactions, children can experience a range of different ways of resolving conflict. They can see the possible solutions and practise actively listening to others. They can have a go at speaking up in a situation which is not personally threatening. Role-play situations provide children with opportunities to practise responses that they may later use in conflict situations.

Teacher considerations

How do you respond in conflict situations? Are you able to speak about your concerns and ideas? Can you listen empathetically to others? Do you avoid the conflict by saying nothing? Do you become angry and unable to speak because of your feelings? Keep a logbook of conflict situations and note your responses to them. Were there alternative ways to react? It is a powerful teaching strategy to discuss your own conflicts and ways of resolving them with your children.

As well as monitoring our own conflict resolution strategies, it is worth monitoring the interactions of children in conflict situations. Allowing children to reflect on their own behaviors will enable them to begin to consider other ways of responding to conflicts. If children can only respond aggressively or submissively, they will need to practise other ways of interacting with people. Discuss with children why this is necessary. What 'real life situations' call for a range of conflict resolution strategies?

What you will need

- conflict scenarios such as those in Activity 2.8.
- video recorder (optional)

What to do

1 Ask the children to form groups of three. Provide each group with a conflict scenario.

2 Ask them to consider who would be involved in the conflict and how each character might respond. They can present their role-play before a small audience or the whole class.

3 The teacher or any member of the audience can then ask them to 'take two'. When this happens they must re-enact this scenario to create a different outcome; that is, their characters will use different responses to the conflict, e.g. assertive, aggressive or submissive responses (see Activity 2.8 for definitions).

4 If children cannot re-enact the scenario from a new perspective, another class member can take over.

5 This re-enacting can continue so that many possibilities are explored.

6 Use the role-plays as a basis for brainstorming a long list of possible solutions to the conflict.

Gender dimensions

- How did the boys and girls initially role play their responses to the conflict scenarios?
- Were there children who were only able to respond aggressively?
- Were there children who were able to use assertive statements well?
- Which children displayed active listening skills? How were these acknowledged?

Adaptations

- Read out the scenarios to the whole class and ask for volunteers to come out to the front and act out one possibility. (Ensure that both girls and boys get a chance to have a go.)
- Video the role-plays to analyse the differences in the responses of boys and girls.
- Ask children to reflect on their own behaviors after this activity. Have them record their reflections to revisit at a later time.

Assertive speaking

Communication:
Moving forward

Now that you have tried a number of activities it is an appropriate time to revisit and reflect on communication skills in the classroom. This section aims to help you to identify possible problems and the implications. Further teaching suggestions are listed to address your concerns and questions about non verbal, active listening and assertive speaking skill development. Some indicators of changed behavior are provided for diagnostic and evaluative purposes.

Non-verbals

What is the problem?

- Children's non-verbal behavior is intimidating others.
- Children do not understand others' feelings or actions.
- Children convey non-verbal messages which may not be intended.

What are the implications?

- Some children (often girls) will not feel comfortable about speaking up.
- Some children feel threatened by others and therefore are silenced.
- Children are misunderstood.

What can be done?

- Use activities which require children to focus on what non-verbal behavior is 'saying'.
- Use a video recorder to watch what is happening when children are working.
- Mime feelings and ideas while others guess the message. Are children getting the right message or are actions misinterpreted. What do we need to take into account?

- Reflect on times when people rely on non-verbal communication to convey a message.
- Involve children in activities which require them to reflect upon how they feel, for example, about their work, progress, interactions.
- Watch a video with the volume turned down. What ideas are conveyed through the images? Why do children understand the ideas differently? Were children influenced by the sex of the (silent) speakers? Replay the section to hear the intended message.

Indications of changed behavior

- Children can interpret non-verbal communication.
- Children are using receptive and appropriate non-verbal behavior.
- Listening skills improve.
- Children are responding more positively to others' ideas.

Where do you go from here?

- Ask children to be involved in more sophisticated forms of reflection which involves metacognitive thinking. For example, after children have reflected on their group behavior, ask them to set their own personal learning goals and assess themselves.
- Ask children to share non-verbal cues that are unique to their cultural background, and find out about their origin.

Active listening

What is the problem?

- Children show little understanding or sympathy toward others.
- Children don't listen to each other. They change the topic, talk about themselves or ridicule the speaker.
- Children cannot restate what has been said.
- Children do not respond to what others have said.
- Children do not value the opinions/feelings of others.

Implications

- Some children's opinions are not heard or valued.
- Many inappropriate ideas are reinforced.
- Some children (usually girls) feel reluctant to speak up.
- Children may feel uncomfortable because they are not used to listening.
- Some boys may react aggressively because they do not like to be ignored.
- Some children insist that their views are heard but do not listen to others.

What can be done?

- Make time for children to practise active listening skills.
- Always acknowledge appropriate listening behavior and encourage children to do the same.
- Ask children to monitor who speaks and who listens. Discuss the fairness and brainstorm ways to change behavior.
- Use reporting back exercises where children are required to rephrase, reword and ask appropriate questions to ensure they 'hear the feelings'. (See Activity 2.4)
- Explain the notion of wait time and how important it is to think before responding to questions and statements.
- Reinforce the importance of non-verbal communication.
- Teach and practise strategies which require children to:
  - stick to the speaker's topic
  - resist analysing or criticising the speaker
  - attend to body language
  - ask questions to find out more about the listener's fears and feelings
  - understand the speaker's point of view
  - check facts
  - avoid defensive behavior
  - acknowledge the speaker's viewpoint

(Cornelius & Faine 1989)

Indicators of changed behavior

- Children will be able to rephrase what has been said.
- Children ask appropriate questions of each other.
- More children will become involved in discussions.
- Fewer conflicts will arise (in the long term) because children will learn to understand and appreciate different viewpoints.
- Children show empathy and support towards speakers.

Where do we go from here?

- Compile class lists about what good speakers and listeners do. Regularly revise and add to these as necessary.
- Ask children to monitor their own and others' behavior.
- Ensure that children build assertive speaking skills. Assertive speakers expect to be heard. This is particularly important for girls.
- Offer additional activities to those children (often boys) who have not had prior experience in active listening.

> I leant that you should all way be a good lister. Because the people you are talking to you fell silly, unhappy and lots more. angry,

> I have Learnt that Joel dasent lisen all the time and I falt like riping Joels head off !!!!!

Moving forward

Assertive speaking

What is the problem?

- Some children (particularly girls) do not choose to:
  - report back to their group
  - speak in front of large groups
  - speak in any situation
- Many boys make fun of girls who speak up (inside and outside the classroom).
- Some boys do not listen when girls speak.
- Some children always 'give in' to more outspoken children.
- Some children are unable to speak about their own ideas.

What are the implications?

- Many children do not develop the confidence to speak up for themselves. They are quiet because they feel intimidated.
- Children are not developing important public-speaking skills. This eventually limits their access to powerful positions and their ability to contribute to decision-making processes.
- Not all children's opinions are taken into account. Some boys' interests/needs are heard and responded to more often.
- Stereotyped 'masculine' and 'feminine' behaviors are not challenged and may be reinforced.
- Some children (often girls) do not believe they have the right to speak up and be heard.

What can be done?

- Children can take turns at being the speaker in a variety of situations, for example:
  - reporting for the group
  - class reports
  - answering questions
- Children and teachers can monitor who speaks when and for how long and who the teacher asks to speak or to answer questions.

- Implement a policy of 'wait-time' in the classroom so that all children have a chance to think before you ask for an answer.
- Give children time to develop arguments that assert their opinion.
- Make time for children to understand and practise using 'I' statements.
- Ask children to restate arguments so that facts are stated in a way that is not offensive to anyone.
- Randomly distribute people or occupation role cards to children. Select an issue or conflict to discuss from different standpoints.
- Ask children to reflect on times when people have said things that have upset them. Ask them how they respond. For example, shout, turn off, try to get even, listen to their ideas, react violently, ask questions, call them names or use 'I' statements. Are these reactions a habit? Have children role play these responses from a new perspective which works towards resolving the conflict.

Indications of changed behavior

- Children are allowing others to speak.
- Children are not aggressive or submissive.
- Children are willing to respond without using put-downs.
- An increased number of girls are volunteering to speak.
- Children regularly use 'I' statements.

Where do you go from here?

- Involve children in non-competitive debating where children listen to a range of perspectives.
- Prepare speeches for other classes/parents, etc.
- Ask children to provide feedback to speakers.
- Regularly discuss the importance of active listening and assertive speaking.

Cooperative learning

What is cooperative learning?

Unlike traditional group work, cooperative learning involves sharing responsibility, sharing resources and working toward common goals.

The development of cooperative group skills involves time, practice and reinforcement of appropriate behavior. The teacher plays an important role in establishing a supportive environment, one in which students feel secure to take risks, an environment where all students' opinions are valued.

Cooperative group work can help all learners by enhancing understanding, and promoting enjoyment and positive attitudes towards work and self. But in order for all students to benefit from cooperative group activities, all students need access to a variety of skills and roles. For example, many girls will need experience as reporters and many boys will need experience as scribes. All students need to develop assertive speaking and active listening skills (see the Communication section).

Some children have not learned how to value the ideas of others. This can be particularly obvious when children work in mixed sex groups. Girls will often also accept the ideas of boys (rather than the other way round) to avoid conflict. Many boys tend to dismiss or ridicule the ideas of girls. If some boys continually dominate the talk time, other students miss out on opportunities to speak their ideas and clarify their opinions. How can they become confident in asserting their ideas?

In choosing the different roles for cooperative learning work, it may be fairer (and seem fairer) to draw names, pick colors, keep a 'rotation record', for example, so that everyone has to take responsibility for different tasks over the month and everyone's contributions are encouraged and valued.

It should be noted that some cultures believe that real learning comes from only the teacher and so therefore, do not see the value or the benefits of working in cooperative groups. While differences in preferred learning styles should be acknowledged, the skills children develop through cooperative learning will be useful to them, regardless of their different cultural backgrounds.

Cooperative skills can be most effectively developed within meaningful contexts. Ideally, activities should be integrated with classroom topics, and many activities can be adapted for cooperative groups. Activities that are open-ended and require divergent thinking (such as problem-solving tasks), and that value many viewpoints and allow for alternative outcomes or require sharing resources/tasks are particularly suitable for developing cooperative group skills.

3.1 Build it together

Level K–6

MATHEMATICS/ TECHNOLOGY

Purposes
- to demonstrate the value of working in teams
- to encourage students to share and value each other's ideas
- to facilitate sharing of limited materials
- to consider the elements of strong construction designs

Background information

Teachers are often viewed as the 'expert' who has all the information and whose responsibility is to pass it on through teacher-centred programs. Many children have not experienced or do not understand the value of cooperative work. These expectations need to be explored and the value of cooperative group work explained. By beginning with a discussion of why it is important to learn to work together, some of the concerns about cooperative work can be addressed. Additionally, when cooperative group skills are made explicit, cooperative learning no longer may be viewed as 'a waste of time' or 'not proper teaching'.

Teacher considerations

How confident are you of your own cooperative learning skills? Have you had the opportunity, through working with other teachers or in professional development programs, to explore the skills and the means to develop them for yourself? Remember, cooperative learning is not the same as group work; it is more skill oriented and requires everyone to participate, taking on a particular role in order for the group to complete the joint task.

How can you make explicit to your students the skills involved in cooperative learning? How can you encourage all members to play an active role in the cooperative group? What can you say to the class to make your expectations about sharing roles explicit?

What you will need

- construction material, e.g. newspaper and masking tape, straws and pins, blocks
- rulers

What to do

1 Ask cooperative groups to design and make a construction that is at least ... (specify dimensions) that will pass the block test (i.e. must be freestanding and steady when a block is placed on it).

2 Encourage children to talk (or brainstorm) about possible designs before collecting materials and beginning their designs.

3 After constructions have been put to the block test, ask group reporters to explain how their group decided on how to build their construction and the way that they worked together; for example, How did you ensure that everyone had a say?

Gender dimensions

- Were both males and females active participants in the design process? Did some of the boys take over? Did some of the girls sit back and watch?
- Were materials distributed fairly?
- Who was chosen as the reporter and how was this person chosen? How many groups chose a male reporter?
- How well did children encourage the participation of other group members?

Adaptations

- Select different materials.
- Put a time limit on construction.
- Ask children to have a drawn design approved by you before construction starts.
- Have students start planning and building before they embark on group work.

Cooperative learning

Level K–6

LANGUAGE AND LITERATURE

3.2 The Paperbag Princess: story map

Purpose
- to explore with children portrayals of male and female characters in a counter-sexist fairy story
- to examine how the characters are created in order to be different from those in traditional stories
- to develop children's skills in mapping storylines
- to enhance children's skills in working in cooperative groups

Background information

The Paperbag Princess is a non-traditional or counter-sexist story. While it shares some of the characteristics of traditional fairy tales, for example, the main characters include a princess, a prince and a rampaging dragon, the story challenges the usual storyline by having the princess 'save' the prince through the use of cleverness rather than killing. There are other clear differences in that the princess is portrayed as active and competent, unconcerned about her appearance, and the ending is not 'marriage and happily ever after'.

The Paperbag Princess challenges the traditional fairy story by suggesting that princesses (girls) are not always helpless, that they too can play powerful parts, and that appearance is not the most significant thing for all princesses (girls). While simply reading and discussing the story does not mean that girls and boys will automatically accept these ideas, presenting girls as competent and powerful encourages children to consider these possibilities as acceptable ways of behaving.

The story proposes some new options for everyone who reads it and indirectly gives recognition to the ways in which some girls demonstrate different understandings of what they mean by 'feminine' behaviors. However, some children will resist this reading of the story and insist, for example, that princesses can't save anyone. Their perspectives need to be listened to and sensitively addressed. While respecting and valuing difference, we can encourage children to consider other possibilities.

Teacher considerations

Can you think of a time in your own life when you have acted 'powerfully' to help someone else? How was your assistance received? Is it harder for a male to accept help from a female, do you think? Why/why not?

What do you like/dislike about the story? What traditional assumptions are being played with? How do you respond to the princess/the prince?

What you will need

- at least one copy of *The Paperbag Princess*
- large sheets of butchers paper
- drawing materials

What to do

1 Read the story to the class.

2 Discuss the storyline and characters.

3 Group the children into mixed groups of approximately 4–5 and ask them to decide who will take the responsibility for being the recorder, the reporter, the timekeeper, the task-keeper, the encourager.

4 The group task is to design a story map that shows the sequence of major events in the story. Groups need to decide how the task will be organised and presented. (Students will often decide to divide the story into parts, and then illustrate a part each before joining the map together.)

5 Each group reports back to the whole group on their story map.

6 Ask each group to comment on how well individuals listened, contributed, completed their task and what could be done to improve the way the group worked.

Gender dimensions

- Are there differences between how the girls and the boys respond?
- Are there differences among the girls in what they say about the princess and the prince?
- From your own observations and from what each group had to say, did particular boys take up most of the talking time? Who were they? Did they realise this?

Cooperative learning

- Did particular girls actively contribute to the group discussion? Were their contributions acknowledged and valued in the same way that the boys' contributions were? By whom?
- Who took which roles? Are the roles of the cooperative group shared around or do some children always take the same roles?

Adaptations

- Select other literature as a basis of a story mapping activity. Compare the more traditional storylines with the counter-sexist stories (see Further Reading). Have the children compare and contrast the different story maps. How are these alike? different?
- Using story maps as a starting point, have children collaborate in writing non-traditional stories. Discuss what they like/dislike about these.

Further reading

Blackwood, M. & Argent, K. 1987, *Derek the Dinosaur*, Omnibus Books, Sydney.

Graham, B. 1987, *Crusher Is Coming*, Lothian, Melbourne.

Hilton, N. 1987, *The Long Red Scarf*, Omnibus Books, Sydney.

Mahy, M. 1985, *Jam*, Dent, London.

Munch, R. 1980, *The Paperbag Princess*, Pinnacle Press, Toronto.

Trialling comments

This activity was trialled in a year 3/4 classroom. A lot of time was spent discussing the differences between this story and other fairy tales. When children were asked to describe the prince and princess, they described the princess as pretty and the prince as strong. They 'read' the story quite differently from the teacher. Other teachers have found that children interpret Ronald as homosexual.

Level 3–6

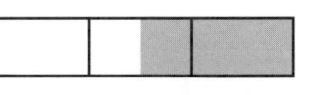

3.3 Create a slogan

ART/LANGUAGE

Purposes
- to begin to examine the way advertisements simplify ideas in order to sell products
- to consider the images of females and males as portrayed in advertisements
- to develop with children an understanding of how the media sells a product
- to enhance children's skills in sharing ideas, actively listening and reaching consensus
- to encourage active group discussion
- to practise drawing and design skills

Background information

Children often watch many hours of television. In the process, they glean an understanding of how this medium works to sell particular products; many children are able to recite advertising slogans verbatim, and can often sing the accompanying tunes for their favorite breakfast cereal or soft drink, for example. While we may worry about children 'soaking up' such 'mindless' information, we can also use their expertise as a way of helping them to 'deconstruct' what the media is doing, how it operates to sell particular products.

Advertisements 'work' because they appeal to a particular audience. They often portray boys as the active sex and girls as the ones who will 'naturally' prefer to play with dolls and make-up. Girls often report a feeling of 'unfairness' about the limits placed on their possibilities, especially related to sporting products and activities. Boys are more likely to resist the notion of crossing traditional feminine and masculine borders.

By examining advertisements that they like, girls and boys can reach a better understanding of the way in which advertisements simplify, beautify, exemplify and induce people to buy the product. They can also develop a healthy understanding about the difference between the world of advertisements and their own worlds.

Cooperative learning

Teacher considerations

Think of an advertisement that you like. What appeals to you? How are females portrayed in this advertisement? How are males presented? Is it based on stereotypical assumptions about women or about men? Is humor used? How is music used?

Suspend your own value system in asking children to comment on their favorite advertisements. What is it that they like? The visuals? The music? The product itself? What appeals to them as children? As girls? As boys? Do students from different cultural backgrounds like different advertisements?

What you will need

- drawing materials
- large sheets of butchers paper
- magazines for reference

What to do

1 Ask children to name their favorite advertisements. What is it that they like about them? What products are being advertised? Who are the 'characters' in these advertisements? Who would buy these products? How do the children 'know' this?

2 Discuss with children the use of slogans. For example, 'The Real Thing: Coke'; or 'You ought to be congratulated ...' (use examples that the children have named). Why do these slogans 'work'? Why have a few words to stand for the product?

3 Ask the children to divide into groups of about 4–5. Each group is required to design: a) a new product that will appeal to their age level; b) an advertising slogan to sell the product. Remind the groups that every member is expected to participate and the entire group must reach consensus as to the product and the advertising slogan.

4 Each group must be able to explain to the rest of the class why they think their product will appeal to their age level and why their slogan will 'work'. (The task of the recorder is essential.)

5 When each group has completed the task, they will share their ideas with the entire class.

Gender dimensions

- Are there identifiable differences between what the girls like and the boys like in advertising? How might these differences be summed up?
- Were children able to identify stereotyped images?
- Was aggression or violence featured in the advertising designed by children? How can you comment on this?

Adaptations

- Specify the product.
- Ask for the design to be environmentally friendly.
- Ask groups to list ways that the product is attractive to women and/or to men.
- Ask children to make a list of characteristics of male and female images. Discuss: Are these accurate? Why do such images continue to be used?

3.4 Collective cloze

Level K–6

LANGUAGE

Purposes
- to make explicit the use of semantic, syntactic and graphophonic cues for reading
- to use the brainstorming technique to highlight the benefits of working with others

Background information

Because of traditional gendered expectations, females have often been delegated to support roles. Males have often been expected and expect to take on 'up front' roles such as speaker, reporter, chair of meetings. Many females feel that this is unfair; some males do too. Females are often given (and many feel more comfortable with) roles such as recorder and illustrator. Self-selection of roles can be used but the teacher may need to allocate roles to ensure that we allow all children to experience all roles and so develop the necessary range of skills that males and females all need.

Teacher considerations

When working with other adults what sort of feedback do you give? How do you feel when your ideas are criticised? How can you model good feedback? What will you do if students criticise each other's ideas?

What you will need

- passage from a book with words covered up (1 copy per group)
- writing materials

What to do

1 Choose a passage from a familiar book and white out or cover up some words and parts of words. Give one copy to each group of four.

2 Ask groups to appoint a reader, recorder, reporter and timekeeper.

3 Ask groups to brainstorm a list of words for each space. They must make sense semantically and syntactically.

Gender dimensions

- Were all team members' contributions valued equally?
- Did both boys and girls encourage each other?
- Who played the role of the recorder?
- How were roles allocated? Was everyone happy with their role?

Adaptations

- Choose a passage from an unknown text (more difficult task).
- Use students' written work as a basis of the cloze activity. White out or cover up particular/parts of words to reinforce certain skills; for example, adjectives only.
- Use Activity 3.5 to follow up this activity.

3.4 Jumble and unjumble

Level K–6

SOCIAL EDUCATION/ LANGUAGE

Purposes
- to explore the features of sentence structure
- to highlight benefits of collective expertise
- to encourage children to take up a range of roles in a cooperative group

Background information

This simple cooperative exercise enables children to share and clarify their individual understandings of sentence structures, and to assist the group as a whole to come up with the correct answers. The expertise of children who are more skilled in the area can be shared to help other group members who may not be as adept. Allocating different roles — for example, recorder, timekeeper, facilitator — will ensure that everyone has a task to do within the group, that no one person is left out and that some group members do not simply take over.

When the activity is completed, it is worth taking time to discuss with the children how they reached their answers. How did they come to the decisions about correct sentence structure? By making explicit the 'clues' used, children can gain a better understanding of language and how context helps to make meaning.

Teacher considerations

When do you personally actively engage in activities with other teachers? What do you enjoy about the process? What kind of environment do you find necessary before you are able to participate freely? How can you encourage active participation by all children?

What you will need

- strips of paper with sentences on them (1 per group)
- scissors
- textas or other writing materials

What to do

1 Write sentences on strips of paper (or ask children to do so in order to practise their handwriting) and cut the sentences into words.

2 Give each group (of 3–4 children) a different sentence.

3 Ask groups to reconstruct the sentence so that it makes sense.

4 Sentences can be rotated between groups.

5 Emphasise the process of re-creating the sentence that makes sense rather than the speed at which it was completed.

Example for lower grade

We made chocolate crackles.

Example for middle grade

Today we made chocolate crackles after lunch.

Example for upper grade

After talking about ways to share roles we made chocolate crackles after lunch.

Gender dimensions

- Who manipulated the pieces?
- Did children listen to each other's suggestions?
- Did competent girls take over and do most of the work?
- How were the different roles allocated?

Adaptations

- Use children's own writing as a source of sentences.
- To make the task more difficult, cut some words into pieces or individual letters. (Level 2–6)

Cooperative learning

3.6 Body sculpture

Level K–6

PHYSICAL EDUCATION

Purposes
- to promote trust
- to facilitate group laughter
- to encourage children to support each other physically
- to work towards a shared goal
- to demonstrate the use of group skills in a physical activity

Background information

This activity encourages girls and boys to work together in order to accomplish the task: supporting each other physically so that only a set number of 'body parts' touch the ground in their body sculpture. Before doing this, it is important that there is a degree of mutual trust and group cohesiveness already established.

For the first few times, children may choose to work in same sex pairs, or the teacher may assign the pairs. However, encouraging the children to try working with different partners, in girl–boy pairs, can be done by using diverse ways of pairing; for example, it might be worth asking them to find a partner on the basis of the first letter of their name, or on the basis of different heights. This will help to mix the boys and the girls without appearing to force them to do so only on the basis of sex. If children continue to resist, it may be useful to discuss why you think it is important for them to learn to play together as a means of getting to know each other.

It may also be necessary to monitor the degree of rough play when the pairs are working together. If there is too much pushing and shoving, building a body sculpture is less fun for everyone. This provides the group with a chance to talk about how important it is to play in a way in which no one gets hurt and no one feels threatened by aggressive actions. Indirectly, it challenges the idea that the only way to have a good time is to play roughly or aggressively.

Teacher considerations

Do you engage in cooperative or competitive team games? What do you enjoy, find satisfying about each kind? What skills do you see as being unique to each? How do you encourage children to work cooperatively with others?

What you will need

- mats or large outdoor grassed space

What to do

1 Ask children to work in mixed-sex pairs, or use a grouping strategy to ensure that this happens. It is important that group trust has been established. (It may be worth revisiting some of the group-building activities if there are problems.)

2 Have children work together to create body sculptures. For example, the teacher calls out the number three, and in pairs, children create a sculpture where only three body parts are touching the ground. Children need to support each other to create the structure.

3 Take time to have pairs demonstrate their creative ideas in front of the rest of the class.

Gender dimensions

- Who were the children who cooperated well with each other? How was this acknowledged by you? By other members of the group?
- Were there children who found this a difficult activity to do? Why might this be so?
- Who were the risk-takers?

Adaptations

- Start the activity individually, then work in small groups.
- Build towers and other body constructions with larger groups.

Trialling comments

Teachers were surprised how well the children worked during this activity. They noted that some children needed more time to warm to the idea but many groups were imaginative. Some boys did not like sitting or standing near girls. They moved away if girls got close.

3.7 Guess and check

Level K–4

MATHEMATICS

Purposes
- to encourage children to share and justify their ideas
- to promote the practice of listening to everyone's point of view in a group
- to practise making considered judgements about space

Background information

This activity is based on group consensus; while individual guesstimates are called for, the group as a whole must decide on only one answer before testing it. The reasons for each individual's guesstimate need to be listened to closely so that the group can weight up the reasons and achieve consensus.

Some girls and many boys will have prior experience of working with blocks and so therefore may be better at predicting how many blocks will fit. Sharing the expertise is an important aspect in achieving a group decision. Not only will prior experience be important, but the ability to explain why a particular answer makes sense is also vital. Groups should be encouraged to examine the reasons for deciding to go with a particular answer. Did they make sense? What convinced the group that one answer was better than the others?

Teacher considerations

When was the last time that you had to reach a consensus decision with your colleagues? What did you find difficult about the process? Did you feel that your ideas were listened to? Were there other members of the group to whom you deferred because of their prior expertise? What skills are needed in order to reach consensus? What do you find frustrating about the process? How important is this skill for reaching decisions with which everyone can feel comfortable?

What you will need

- regular blocks such as Unifix
- containers such as icecream containers or milk cartons

What to do

1 Divide the class into groups of 4–5, preferably mixed sex.
Ask each group to guess the number of blocks that will fit into their container.

2 Each group must select a recorder to make a note of the guesses, a reporter, and a timekeeper — everyone in the group must agree on one answer before they start to check. The final guessed score should be the product of a group discussion which has involved everyone fairly.

3 Groups might also decide to appoint someone to take the role of manipulator and counter. Encourage groups to ensure that everyone has a role to play.

4 When each group has agreed on an answer, they can test the prediction by counting up the blocks as they go into the container.

5 Have each group report back on how they reached their decision and on how close their final answer was to the actual number of blocks that fit into the container.

6 Ask each group to reflect on the process they went through to achieve the one answer. Was each group member's guesstimate considered? What worked well for the group?

Gender dimensions

- Who took on which roles?
- How were roles allocated?
- Were there some children who found it difficult to listen to other's ideas?
- Were there members of the group who became frustrated when their consensus decision proved inaccurate?
- Did the children value the process as well as the answer?

Adaptations

- Change the materials.
- Calculate perimeter or area.

Cooperative learning

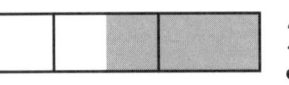

Level 3–6

LANGUAGE

3.8 Newspaper reconstruction

Purposes
- to practise working together in a large group to complete a collaborative task
- to listen to others' ideas
- to examine the features and consider the sequence of a newspaper
- to use logic skills to reconstruct the newspaper

Background information

This activity is for a large group, and assumes that the children will have had prior experience in listening to each other and speaking assertively as individuals. Because of this, it can help you to assess how well individual children are able to work as members of a large group. It may also highlight areas where the group needs to go back and focus again on particular skills, for example, actively listening to everyone's contributions and reaching group agreement.

Teacher considerations

Consider your role when working cooperatively in groups; are there situations when you feel intimidated about speaking in large groups, offering your arguments concerning a particular issue or idea? If so, what can you do about it? What skills do you feel confident that you have?

Are you able to present your ideas in a coherent fashion so that other people will understand them? Do you worry about what others might think of you? If you feel this way, how might the quiet, more reticent children feel about working within a large group? How can you enable others to listen actively and to speak assertively in order to reach group agreement?

What impact do your preferred learning and teaching styles have on your teaching? How much responsibility do you have for meeting the preferred learning styles of children in your class?

What you will need

- a newspaper and a large space

What to do

1 Pull a newspaper apart and give one sheet to each class member (not in order and with the page numbers cut off).

2 Explain to the children that they need to reconstruct the newspaper on the floor in the correct sequence.

3 Each child will need to explain the reasons for placing a particular page in a particular place. The group will need to decide whether they agree with the reasons given before accepting the sequence.

Gender dimensions

- Which children were able to speak assertively and to convince others of their reasons for placing their page in a particular order? Were there differences between girls' and boys' skills in this area?
- Who were the children who were able to listen to others' suggestions?
- Were there any children who criticised others? How did the group deal with their concerns?

Adaptations

- Allow time for children to browse through the newspaper to examine the usual layout first. Discuss with them why particular topics are located on the front pages and others are relegated to the back pages.
- Give children only a few pieces of the newspaper and time their efforts working together to reconstruct the paper.

Trialling comments

Several teachers reported that boys took on the 'directing' roles. Girls were told to collect the materials while the boys waited for the pages to be brought to them. Boys initiated the sequence and took over.

Children talking about where the newspaper pages should be placed. This activity relies on a lot of talking, listening, cooperation and problem-solving.

Cooperative learning

Cooperation:
Moving forward

Now that you have tried a number of cooperative learning activities, it is an appropriate time to revisit and reflect on team work. This section aims to assist you to identify possible classroom relationship problems and the implications. Further teaching suggestions are listed to address your concerns and questions. Some indicators of changed behavior are provided for diagnostic and evaluative purposes.

What is the problem?

- Some children are acting aggressively or submissively.
- Girls do all the work and boys take the credit.
- Children are unwilling to take risks.
- Some children's ideas are being devalued or ignored.
- Children are doing the same roles time and time again. For example, many girls are always the recorders and the ones who collect the materials, while some boys are often the speakers and seem to control what happens in the groups.
- Some children dominate group work while others rarely say anything or appear disinterested.
- Girls often appear passive. They give in if differences of opinions arise.
- Boys take over the resources.
- Some children play up or refuse to participate in group tasks.
- Children put others down. This usually happens to quiet boys and girls.

What are the implications?

- Children do not speak up regularly in groups, therefore they do not receive positive feedback about their ideas or stimulation to rethink.

- Many children do not develop confidence to have a go.
- If behavior continues and is unchallenged, children learn to think that this is what is expected of them. We can be reinforcing inappropriate group behavior.
- Cooperative group work is not a positive or worthwhile experience for all children.
- Cooperative group work can disempower girls.

What can be done?

- Model risk-taking. Tell children explicitly when you are doing so, your reasons and how you feel.
- When possible, work in a team yourself. Show children that cooperative group learning works for you and that it is important for all people to be able to work in groups. Always demonstrate active listening and assertive speaking.
- Make a list of encouraging things to do and say to other class members.
- Discuss how it feels to give and receive constructive and positive feedback.
- Ask children to write encouraging letters to others praising them on certain aspects of cooperative group behavior.
- Do not allow dominating, harassing and aggressive behavior to continue unchallenged. Approach this in a consistent way which models peaceful conflict resolution strategies.
- Ensure that the tasks are appropriate for cooperative group work. For example, they are open ended, value different ideas and can be divided into smaller tasks or roles.
- Generate a list of roles for each student. The teacher or children can distribute these. Make sure children have a clear understanding of their role and the task. (Ensure that children have experienced a range of roles such as reporter, recorder, noise monitor, time-keeper, encourager.)
- Role cards may need to be given to younger or inexperienced children to ensure that everyone knows what their job is.
- Carefully choose group members.

- Assess and give feedback to the whole team (not individuals). Note: There are times when it is appropriate to give feedback to individuals about their work in groups.

- Ask children to reflect regularly on cooperative group work. What do they think is working well and what would they like to improve? Some of these reflections may be shared with the class.

Indications of changed behavior

- Roles are being shared more fairly in cooperative group work.
- Role-taking will develop new skills in both girls and boys.
- Children are taking turns at listening and speaking.
- Differences of opinion are seen as important to learning rather than something to be put down.
- More children are enjoying cooperative group work.
- Children will be more willing to take a risk and others will congratulate and encourage this behavior.
- Children see the purpose and value in cooperative group work.
- Girls and/or other previously quiet members of the group will gain confidence.
- Both girls and boys will share the power of owning materials and products.
- Harassment, aggressive and dominant behavior will diminish in the long term.

Where do you go from here?

- Allow children to decide which roles are appropriate for certain tasks.
- Regularly review behaviors which contribute to and hamper cooperation. Make class charts of these so that they are always on display.
- Introduce more challenging group tasks. These could be extended investigations (some examples are given in the next section).
- As well as self and group assessment, peer assessment could be used to monitor group interactions (see Blackline Masters 1, 2 and 3).

Problem-solving and negotiation

The activities in this section act as starting points for combining and practising the skills of active listening, assertive speaking and cooperative learning. Like these skills, negotiation and problem-solving are skills which we all need and use on a daily basis. However, real negotiation cannot occur unless the skills of active listening, assertive speaking and cooperation are practised as well.

Negotiating a solution using many ideas often results in a better solution than if only one or two ideas are used. In fact, negotiation usually demonstrates that the 'whole is greater than the sum of its parts'.

It is very important that time is spent in exploring as many ideas/solutions as possible rather than choosing the first or second solution that comes to mind. A useful rule of thumb is to come up with at least seven possibilities. Many people move too quickly to compromise, which is often a solution that meets only some of the stated needs. It is often possible to find a solution to many problems which satisfies everyone without resorting to compromise. The process of brainstorming, generating as many ideas as possible regardless of feasibility, is a necessary and important stage in negotiation. Brainstorming has been used in a number of the earlier activities as well.

Like the skills explored in the earlier sections, the skills of negotiation and problem-solving need to be practised often and discussed frequently in order for children to develop confidence in the process and to achieve successful outcomes. The following activities are examples which can be adapted or extended in many ways.

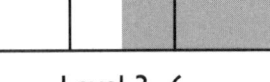

Level 3–6

LANGUAGE

4.1 Design and write a children's book

Purpose
- to explore with children the process involved in writing a children's book
- to investigate how different books are written for different audiences
- to provide an opportunity for children to work cooperatively in order to begin developing negotiation skills
- to encourage children to share their knowledge and expertise with younger children

Background information

Because of gendered expectations, many girls will have experience in looking after younger children. This helps them to develop the important and essential skills of caring for and nurturing others. Many boys do not always have the opportunity to gain these important skills. Nevertheless, as adults they too will need to know how to communicate with, and care for, children and others.

This activity recognises the knowledge of children who have previous experiences of working with younger siblings while providing an opportunity for those who have not been expected to take responsibility for caring for others to gain a better understanding of younger children. It builds on the cooperative learning skills introduced in the previous section and provides an opportunity for girls and boys to work together in practising their active listening and assertive speaking skills.

The activity provides children with the opportunity of sharing their creative ideas and developing them together. The chance to read their children's book to younger children provides them with an audience for their work. It can also be risk-taking in that they have invested their time and ideas in creating this book which will be offered to an audience for approval. It may be worth considering with children the feelings that this can evoke: anxiety, disappointment, pleasure, satisfaction.

Teacher considerations

Do you enjoy writing, drawing, painting? Have you written and/or illustrated books? Do you like to work alone or with others in your creative pursuits? What do you enjoy about working alone? working with others? What are some of the difficulties with each? Do you share your endeavors with others or is the pleasure gained from the creation enough? How confident do you feel in showing your work to others?

What you will need

- whiteboard, blackboard or butchers paper for the class chart
- art paper for children to use for illustrations and text of their book
- agreement from another teacher in a younger grade for time to have the story books read to their children (optional)

What to do

This activity will take a number of sessions and so has been broken down into parts. However, it may be possible to combine or to skip some of these, depending on how the activity is progressing, the age of the group you are working with, and how able the children are in undertaking the various steps.

Part 1

As a whole class or in small groups, discuss:
- Who reads children's books?
- What do you understand by 'children's books'?
- Who is the audience for children's books?
- How do children's books cater for the interests of children?
- On the basis of their responses, create a class chart: A Recipe For a Good Children's Book.

Part 2

Have the children bring from home or borrow from the library a collection of children's books. It may be easier to target a particular age group: books that 7-year-olds would enjoy, or picture books for 5-year-olds, etc. In small groups, have the children analyse several of the books: consider the kinds of characters that are used; what happens in the storyline. Is there dialogue? What do they like or dislike about the illustrations? How do these books appeal to their audience? Are some topics more appropriate for different age groups than others?

Part 3

In small groups, have the children create their own children's book. Decide who the audience will be, on the basis of who their stories will be read to: Preps? Year Ones? Year Threes? Each group must decide on characters and how the storyline will develop and how the story will be illustrated, keeping the age range of their audience in mind. Once the group has discussed and negotiated about their book, they then must decide who will take responsibility for what part. Groups may decide to work through all of the above together or to allocate the different jobs. Alternatively, groups and roles may be assigned by the teacher. However they choose to work, remind each group that they must all agree on the above ideas before beginning the work.

Part 4

As each group designs and writes their story, set aside time to conference along the way about how each member of the group is contributing. What still needs to be done? Who will do what? It may be useful to negotiate a timetable so that steady progress is made in finishing the story before the due date.

Part 5

When the books are completed and the children are satisfied with their illustrations and texts, members of each group can organise to have the story read to a younger child. This may be a visit to a younger class in the school or children can read their stories to younger brothers and sisters. The reader(s) should take the responsibility of discussing the story and illustrations with the younger children. What did they like? What did they find most interesting? How would they like the story to be changed? The reader(s) can then report back to their group on how their book was received by an audience.

Part 6

In the same small groups, assess each member's contributions. How did the group work together? What worked well? What could be done to improve the way the group functioned? Self-assessment and peer assessment could be used to assist the discussion concerning the group skills. (See Blackline Masters 1 and 2).

Gender dimensions

- Did girls and boys choose to work together?
- How did the members of each group decide on the characters and storyline? Were some children's ideas ignored without discussion?
- How were disagreements settled?
- Were the main characters created for the stories more often male or female?
- Did the children follow gender stereotypes or were they able to generate many different activities for their characters?
- Were the illustrations more often done by girls or by boys?
- What images did they portray?

Adaptations

- Invite an author or illustrator of children's books to talk to the class about how they work. Have the children draw up a list of questions before the speaker comes concerning information they would like to learn about writing and/or illustrating books. The children may wish to show their stories to the speaker for comments.
- Invite parents and other grades in to the class for a book launch.

The children are working together to reach agreement.

Problem-solving and negotiation

4.2 Dinosaur dilemma

Level K–6

LANGUAGE/ DRAMA

Purpose
- to explore individual differences with children
- to provide practice in assertive speaking and active listening
- to practise negotiation and problem-solving skills
- to challenge children to make predictions about text using illustration cues
- to encourage children to translate written text into oral text
- to explore understandings about 'appropriate' masculine and feminine behaviors and how such understandings may be related to cultural difference

Background

Often the beliefs children bring to the classroom about 'appropriate' behaviors are based on stereotyped assumptions about what boys should do and what girls should do. Many times these behaviors are categorised as sets of separate or oppositional behaviors, for example 'boys don't cry — girls do'; 'girls can't play football — boys can'. Unless challenged, these understandings can limit the shared experiences of children and can result in rejection of those children who don't always fit into particular modes of behavior. Individual differences and diversity are vital concepts for children to understand and to respect.

Derek the Dinosaur tells the story of Derek and his friend Montmorency, the mouse. Unlike his ferocious and 'typical' dinosaur brothers, Derek enjoys a quiet life of knitting and cooking although he sometimes worries that he isn't like his brothers. A dramatic change in the weather, however, sends his brothers to Derek for help and he is able to provide them with his knitted scarves and mittens so they are saved from the sudden change to a cold climate.

The book is interesting because it challenges some traditional assumptions (e.g. appropriate behavior for male dinosaurs) and contains themes about: friendships based on difference rather than sameness; the importance of everyone's different contributions; the value of sharing with others; the possibility of enjoying non-typical activities and the worries associated with being different.

While all the characters are written as male, and the generic (exclusive) term 'man' is used in the first sentence, these can provide a way to begin or to continue to explore with children assumptions about language and stereotypes of male/female behaviors: In telling this story, why would the author use only male dinosaurs? How does this work in the story? What is understood by the word 'man'? Is there another/better word available? How do the girls feel about reading a book where there are no female characters? What books have boys read recently with only female characters? Does the sex of the character matter? Why/why not?

Some children, girls as well as boys, may resist the idea that it is okay for a male to knit, to make tea and biscuits, etc. because this does not fit with their own understandings of appropriate masculine behaviors. It is important to hear what they have to say, to be sensitive to their concerns; it is also worthwhile exploring their assumptions with them, not in a 'right answer, wrong answer' way but through an approach that considers acceptance of differences and an openness to alternative possibilities.

Teacher considerations

Do you crochet or knit or embroider? Do you know of any (other) males who do? Why are these fine arts seen as belonging mainly to women? What assumptions underpin these stereotypes? If these art/craft forms are viewed as skills which many people (males as well as females) can benefit from and enjoy, how can the assumptions about 'appropriate' behaviors be challenged? How can the skills be taught in such a way that they are valued for the enjoyment, product and the beauty produced?

What you will need

- a copy of *Derek the Dinosaur* by Mary Blackwood and Kerry Argent (1987, Omnibus)

What to do

1 Cover the title and all text in the book. (This can be done by paper-clipping or taping blank sheets of paper over the text so that only the illustrations can be seen.)

2 Tell the children that you will show them the illustrations only, and together they will try to work out what the storyline is.

3 If using this with older children, ask one or two children to act as recorders for the various suggestions that the group will make.

4 Discuss the cover illustration: what might this story be about? Point out that the main character is a green dinosaur. (It might be worth asking the children to choose a name for the dinosaur.) Work through the illustrations with them, drawing attention to what is happening in each picture.

5 Accept all the suggestions offered, and ask children to explain what clues they found to make them decide. (For example, if they decide that the green dinosaur is female, ask them what makes them think that is true. If they decide it is male, ask for clarification.)

6 When they have finished deciding, go over the various suggestions which the recorders have written down. There could be many different interpretations — depending on how different children 'read' the illustrations for cues.

7 Next, uncover the text and read the story as it is written. Compare the author's story with the ideas that the children have proposed. What surprised them about the story? What assumptions did they make on the basis of the activities that Derek is shown doing (e.g. knitting, pouring tea, hanging up clothes, etc). What expectations did they have about dinosaurs (male and female)?

The author decided to create a dinosaur who liked doing different activities from his brothers. Point out that because of his different skills, he was able to save his brothers' lives.

8 Discuss: Why did Derek worry about not being like his brothers? Why did he continue to knit? How important was having a friend like Montmorency? How was Derek able to use his skills to help others?

9 Ask the children individually to list the activities/hobbies they enjoy doing. Have them share their lists with others. What likes do they share in common with others? Are there some which they enjoy but which their friends don't? What would the world be like if everyone did exactly the same activities? What would be missing?

10 How many of the children know how to knit, crochet, embroider, sew, cook, etc? Who taught them? How important is it for everyone to learn these skills? Why?

Gender dimensions

- How many of the children decided that the dinosaur who knitted must be female?
- How did different boys react to Derek?
- Which children were able to challenge the male–female stereotypes when they made their story suggestions?

Adaptations

- Ask younger children to list or draw all the things Derek was good at.
- Repeat the activity using other books such as *The Long Red Scarf* by Nette Hilton (1987, Omnibus). Ask children to decide what the story is about on the basis of the illustrations only. How do their stories compare with the text? What assumptions do they make about the main character's activities?
- Explore with children where and how knitting, crochet, embroidery, etc. developed. For example, crochet was initially used to make fishing nets. It is probable that mainly men crocheted the nets.
- Teach the children, perhaps with the help of parents, how to knit, crochet, embroider. If some of the girls already know how, pair them with someone else who doesn't. This acknowledges their skills and gives the learners some individual attention. Have the children make gifts for their relatives, e.g. scarves, pot-holders, etc.

Problem-solving and negotiation

4.3 Create a circuit

Level K–6

SCIENCE

Purposes
- to allow children to experiment with materials to create an electric circuit
- to encourage risk-taking
- to involve children in a problem-solving activity
- to practise listening, speaking and cooperative group skills

Background information

Some children will not have had the opportunity to 'play' with equipment like this. Anxiety can be provoked when children (and adults) are asked to do something that they are unfamiliar with, particularly when it involves science materials which many boys see as their territory. It is important for girls as well as boys to gain confidence in the area of problem-solving and tinkering with materials. However, to overcome some students' initial anxiety, using single-sex groups may help to ensure that the less confident also gain the experience. Alternatively, if the team spirit is strong, consider pairing boys and girls together so that one person who feels confident will work with another who is less sure about the task.

Teacher considerations

Hands-on science is engaging — and risky if we haven't had much experience of it. How confident do you feel in undertaking this activity? How much experience have you had in pulling things apart and putting them back together? Some teachers are less than enthusiastic because they themselves have not had the opportunity to explore this kind of science. If you feel less than confident, try practising with another teacher whom you trust and who is willing to share their knowledge with you. Be sure that you do the hands-on — and don't just 'get the answer' from your friend. The process of experimenting is as important as the actual outcome of building a circuit.

What you will need

- batteries, wire and light bulbs

What to do

1 An introductory discussion could be conducted although this need only be short. You might wish to ask children to discuss what they already know about creating a circuit — this could be listed on a class chart and compared later with findings. Alternatively, tell children what resources are available and leave it to them to play with the materials and make their own discoveries.

2 Tell children that they must use the materials to make a circuit and light up the globe.

3 Allow time for children in small groups to experiment with the materials and discuss their ideas about how to construct a circuit.

4 At the end of the session, a whole group discussion could be conducted when children share their problem-solving strategies and cooperative group skills used. If you choose to do this, you could ask that groups appoint a note-taker. Suggest that they note what problems they encountered and how these were solved.

Gender dimensions

- Were some children reluctant to handle the materials? Were girls more cautious than boys?
- If working in mixed groups, did the boys take over?
- What problem-solving strategies did the children use? Were there differences between the ways in which boys and girls approached the task?
- Did the boys do most of the talking and the girls most of the listening? (Consider using a group assessment sheet. See Blackline Master 3).
- How well did the children use their cooperative group skills to complete the task? Ask for an oral or a written reflection on this.

Adaptations

- After completing the activity ask children to draw a cartoon strip demonstrating the process they went through to create their circuit.
- Ask children to reflect on this activity. You could select a focus for this reflection, such as how they felt as they were working, the cooperative group skills and problem-solving strategies used, what they need to improve, etc.

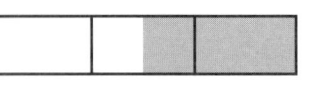

4.4 There's a chance

Level 3–6

MATHEMATICS

Purposes
- to make guesses about chance and probability
- to involve children in a problem-solving activity where they can change their guesses given new information
- to encourage risk-taking
- to discuss the importance of using approximations and mistakes for learning

Background information

This activity emphasises the process of problem-solving rather than right/wrong answers. Working in pairs, children have the opportunity to compare their guesses, share their understandings and renegotiate their answers. This process lessens the fear of failing to find the right answer, explores the processes of probability, and makes taking guesses less personally risky. Many girls and some boys find this open-ended approach more conducive to learning. Again, it is worthwhile encouraging boys and girls to work with different partners to enhance their shared understandings and build up their mutual respect for each other.

Teacher considerations

How do you demonstrate your own ability to learn new skills? your own risk-taking behaviors with children? Are you able to discuss with the children your own understandings about problem-solving? To ensure that children feel confident to take risks, a supportive classroom environment is necessary. How does your classroom environment support risk-taking and creative thinking?

What you will need
- approximately 20 colored counters
- a paper bag which cannot be seen through
- chart for recording guesses (optional)
- Blackline Master 9

What to do

1 Tell children how many counters you have and the colors. For example: 'I have 20 counters altogether. There are some blues, reds, greens and yellows.'

2 Select between 4 and 6 counters at random and put them in the bag. Tell children how many you have selected, but that you have not seen the counters. Do not allow children to see them either.

3 Ask children (in pairs) to write down a guess of the color combination of counters you have in the bag or use the Blackline Master 9.

4 Pick out 1, 2 or 3 counters and show them to the children.

5 Allow children to change their guess now that they know what some of the counters are. For example, if a pair have guessed that there are 2 blues and 2 reds and the first couple of counters you show are yellow and green, they can make their new guess to include yellow and green. Allow time for them to discuss the new guesses.

6 Return counters to the bag and continue the process of showing children a number of counters from the bag (selected randomly) and allowing them to guess the color combinations for a specified number of turns, say 10, or until someone guesses the right combination.

7 Discuss the reasons for changing guesses.

Gender dimensions

- Which children were willing to have a go at guessing the color combinations? Were the boys the first to want to guess?
- Who were the children who changed their guesses when given information conflicting with their guesses?
- Did children display any negative behavior such as booing, hitting, throwing etc. when their guesses were wrong?
- Were the girls and boys willing to take risks in their guesses?

Adaptations

- Change the number of counters shown as clues.
- Change the number of counters put in the bag.
- Allow children to be the teacher, i.e. they select and show the counters put in the bag.
- Record the results of each 'show' on the blackboard to analyse later.

(adapted from C. Chandler 1994, *Dice Don't Have Brains*, MAV, Melbourne)

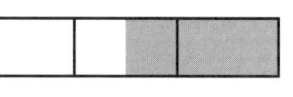

4.5 Represent an issue

Level 3–6

ART/SOCIAL EDUCATION

Purposes
- to practise negotiation and problem-solving skills
- to encourage creative and logical thinking
- to use listening, speaking and cooperative group skills
- to discuss and represent an issue from a number of perspectives

Background information

Through the media and their own experiences, many children are aware of social issues. Unemployment, the environment, natural disasters, refugees, crime, war, etc. receive coverage daily on television and in the news. While simplistic solutions are often presented, the skills of considering the issue from different points of view are necessary and need to be developed.

This activity begins to help children understand that complex social issues are rarely easily or quickly solved. It asks them to work together to represent diverse aspects of a particular issue. It is important that they are reminded that many opinions and ideas can and should be heard and represented. They do not need to find one answer to the problem, but can propose many different solutions. The process of working together is an important one because it provides the experience of hearing each other's points of view.

Small groups of children consider a selected issue in a non-confrontational way, and represent it using art materials. Since the group must decide which issue they will represent and how they will do this, the children will need to practise assertive speaking, active listening and cooperative learning skills. The end product should reflect all group members' points of view. The use of art materials to represent diverse ideas allows children to include a range of responses and to celebrate a variety of different ideas.

Teacher considerations

What social issue do you feel passionate about? Whom do you talk with about it? How do you handle opinions/ideas that don't agree with your own? Are you able to listen to and assess them without outright rejection? Can you see why opinions different from your own are held? How easy is it to respect varying opinions?

What you will need

- a range of 'issues' for the children to choose from
- a variety of art materials such as colored paper and cardboard, scissors, glue, cellophane, crepe paper, drinking straws, newspaper and magazines

What to do

1 Ask the children to choose an issue that can be viewed from a number of different perspectives, for example, the changing environment. (This activity could be integrated into current classroom topics.)

2 Show children the materials you have available for their use.

3 Tell them they have five decisions to make:
- Who will they work with?
- What issue will they focus on?
- What part of the issue, e.g. the problem, the possible solutions, the different points of view about the issue, will they represent?
- How will they represent these?
- Who will present the final product to the whole class?

4 Ask children to discuss these decisions before they start work. Remind them to use their active listening and assertive speaking skills.

Gender dimensions

- Who did the children choose to work with? Did most children choose to work with others of the same sex or did they choose team members because of recognised skills?
- What issues were selected? Were they of interest to all group members or only a few? What range of views were presented? Did they show thought and understanding or were they simplistic?
- Did more boys or girls present the groups' final products?
- Did children listen to all team members before making decisions about what issue to represent and how to represent their issue?

Adaptations

- Limit the materials.
- Select issues or brainstorm the possibilities before children break into groups.
- Select working groups yourself.

Problem-solving and negotiation

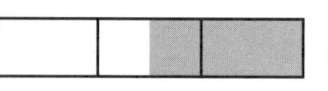

4.6 Imagine a world

Level 3–6

ENVIRONMENTAL SCIENCE

Purposes

- to hear a range of different ideas and opinions
- to practise listening and speaking skills
- to practise negotiation and problem-solving skills in the context of a cooperative environmental science activity
- to encourage creativity

Background information

While the importance of science as an area of study has been increasingly emphasised at primary and post-primary schools, the way in which science relies on team work and creativity to come up with new ideas and new solutions to problems has been less explored. Through this activity, children are encouraged to use their creative and imaginative skills to consider an environmental issue and to share their creativity with others.

This activity also encourages children to consider how other children may have beliefs and values different from their own.

Teacher considerations

How important do you consider environmental education to be? What are your values/beliefs regarding the need to save the rainforests or end the pollution of the air by cars, for example? If you were a farmer/timber worker/politician/car manufacturer, how might your opinions/values be different?

How important do you think it is to listen to people whose opinions/ideas/values are different from your own? How able are you to accept differences in values without feeling the need to challenge or confront those whose ideas are different?

What you will need

- drawing materials
- large pieces of paper

What to do

1 Discuss the environmental issues known to children. You could list these on the board. Alternatively, start with a book such as *Window* by Jeannie Baker or *Conservation* by Robert Ingpen and Margaret Dunkle.

2 Ask children to close their eyes and imagine they have the power to create a perfect world for future generations. What would their world look like? What would be the most important thing?

3 Ask the children, in small groups, to share their visions. Have them together consider what they think is necessary for a world in which everyone is happy. Groups need to make a list of ways to decide what items/ideas/goals are important and how these would be achieved.

4 Children can represent their suggestions in any way the group decides. For example, through written instructions, drawings or drama.

Gender dimensions

- How able were the children to imagine a range of different worlds?
- What values were expressed? Were there differences based on gender and/or cultural experiences?
- Did the quieter girls/boys just go along with other students' ideas?
- How were differences of opinion challenged, accepted and negotiated?
- Did some children insist on their right to be heard before others?
- Who were the children who listened well to other team members? How was this acknowledged?
- Were children able to criticise ideas, not people?

Adaptations

- Pose a particular problem for children to solve in any curriculum area.
- Discuss gender issues or other classroom problems. Ask children to consider possible solutions so that all children feel comfortable and happy.
- Select different methods for children to represent their ideas.

References

J. Baker, *Window*, Julia McCrae, London, 1991.
R. Ingpen & M. Dunkle, *Conservation*, Penguin, Melbourne, 1986.

4.7 Workers' negotiation

Level 4–6

**SOCIAL EDUCATION/
DRAMA EXTENDED
INVESTIGATION**

Purposes
- to consider the negotiation skills required in everyday life
- to practise negotiating and compromising in a dramatic way
- to use active listening and assertive speaking skills
- to revisit cooperative group skills

Background information

This activity aims to provide children with the opportunity to see the relevance of the skills they have been developing to a 'real life' situation. Although drama is used to highlight the need for negotiation skills, drawing connections to children's own understandings about the work place and how it operates can help them to see the importance of the skills.

When using role-plays such as this, remember that it is important to spend time at the end debriefing the characters so that children move from the roles they played to reconsideration of their own personal opinions.

Teacher considerations

What do you understand by the term 'negotiation'? In what situations do you negotiate? How able are you to negotiate with your students? How responsible for their own learning are your students? How able are they to negotiate their ideas and to express their concerns to you?

What you will need

- role-play (optional, see Blackline Master 10)
- space for drama activity.

What to do

1 Create a class chart with two columns. On one side, record a list of occupations that require cooperation. On the other side record particular situations which would involve employees in the process of negotiations. Discuss one example such as: A chocolate factory has received a large order to make boxes for Valentine's Day with a two-day deadline. The person in charge needs to negotiate with the floor manager who needs to negotiate with the union representative who needs to negotiate with the shop floor worker to ensure that the job is completed on time. At first each person after the boss says, 'Why, this is impossible!' and they need to then decide together whether in fact the task can be completed, and if so, how they will do it.

2 Tell children that they are going to role-play a situation that requires negotiation in the workplace. (Use the class chart or Blackline Master 10.) All children stand in line and can hear the dialogue/negotiations taking place with the person before them, one at a time.

3 The instruction must travel down (or up) the line of command in order. Only two people can participate in the conversation, i.e. there are to be no interruptions from others. The activity is finished when the negotiations come to a satisfactory conclusion.

4 It is not necessary to perform the negotiations in front of the class but this could be done. A whole class discussion could follow to unpack the skills and tactics used.

5 Ensure that you allow time for children to get out of role.

Gender dimensions

- How confidently did the girls participate in negotiations?
- Did anyone refuse to enter into negotiations? How was this handled by the rest of the group?
- What tactics were used to negotiate? How many solutions were proposed?
- How well did the children listen to each other?

Adaptations

- The roles can be given in advance for students to research.
- Children with the same roles could meet in support groups to discuss what they could negotiate with others next in line. This would ensure that their positions are well thought through and that everyone has something to say. This technique helps build confidence of children who are reluctant speakers.
- Ensure that children rotate through the roles in subsequent role-plays.
- Analyse the power positions in these scenarios. Does it make a difference if the roles are played by males or females, for example: female boss and male worker?
- Have children create scenarios to role play which show other situations where negotiation is important.
- Consider different ways to negotiate the problem.

Source: The Woolly Jumpers Theatrical Group, Victoria.

Problem-solving and negotiation: Moving forward

Now that you have tried a number of problem-solving and negotiation activities, it is an appropriate time to revisit and reflect on possible classroom relationship problems and the implications.

What is the problem?

- The process of decision-making is not inclusive.
- Some children are exercising power over others when problems are being solved. Some girls often just accept without question or challenge.
- A range of ideas are not explored before decisions are being made.
- Children are not responding appropriately to others' ideas.
- Conflicts arise (often between girls and boys).

What are the implications?

- Some children do not feel a part of the decision-making process. For example, some girls may not have their say and some boys may not listen to others.
- Group products are not representative of all group members. A lack of commitment to the work and learning can result.
- Children feel their ideas are not important, therefore their contributions in the future may diminish.
- Children feel powerless to affect group decisions and withdraw or act aggressively. Behavior problems can result.
- Confidence can be diminished.
- Important negotiation and problem-solving skills are not practised by all children.

- All possibilities are not explored and the result is narrow minded or limited.
- Solutions which acknowledge a range of ideas are not arrived at.

What can be done?

- Arrange seating so that children sit side by side rather than across from each other when resolving problems.
- Practise brainstorming. Demonstrate the value of accepting all ideas before selecting and eliminating some.
- Before conflict arises, ask children to brainstorm ideas first and then use communication skills to solve the problem so that everybody feels comfortable with the final decision.
- Revise problem-solving strategies before starting the activity.
- Practise responding to ideas rather than criticising people personally. When working in groups appoint an 'idea monitor' to ensure that this happens.
- Get children to write down ideas so that everyone's ideas are acknowledged.
- Discuss how actions and comments make people feel. What positive behaviors can we use to enhance the learning of all students? Model and acknowledge these.
- Use strategies such as role and task sharing to include everyone in activities.
- Use some of the ideas listed under the preceding sections for active listening, assertive speaking and cooperation to ensure that everyone has a fair go.
- Ask children to sign work only if they agree with the decision. If they do not all agree the group will need to explain why.

Indications of changed behavior

- More children will be participating in the process of problem-solving.
- Children will recognise the importance of thinking through a variety of ideas.

- Children will monitor for themselves who is saying what.
- Children will think of creative ways to solve problems.
- Active listening and assertive speaking will become an intrinsic part of group problem-solving.
- Girls and boys will be willing to say assertively if they feel they have not been listened to or if they do not agree with what is being said.
- Brainstorming will become a much used strategy in tasks which require problem-solving and negotiating.
- Boys and girls will encourage and praise each other's ideas.

Where do you go from here?

- Continue to build up children's confidence by involving them in a range of activities where girls and boys from different cultural backgrounds respect each other's ideas.
- Use gender equity issues as a starting point for discussion and problem-solving.
- Always acknowledge children when they use effective communication skills and they cooperate to assist others to learn.
- Model appropriate skills and behavior in your interactions with children.
- Celebrate when your efforts are fruitful!

PART

3

WHERE TO FROM HERE?

A gender inclusive curriculum

A gender inclusive curriculum is one which addresses all teaching and learning arrangements (including the learning environment) that affect student outcomes. It examines understandings of masculinity and femininity and takes into account social constructions of gender. A gender inclusive curriculum is achieved by consciously selecting, reflecting upon and addressing choices about classroom planning, implementation and evaluation. These choices are outlined in detail on pages 128 to 132 and include aspects of curriculum planning such as teaching strategies, skills development, language and assessment practices.

Developing your own gender inclusive activities

All activities have the potential to address issues of gender; we do not have to plan 'special' activities as a separate part of our curriculum. We do need to take time, though, to reflect on various aspects of our teaching to ensure that our program promotes gender equity and that it develops skills necessary for relationships based on respect and friendship. We encourage you to design your own gender inclusive activities which are appropriate to your children and program.

Some generic key questions which may be used to guide reflections and observations in any classroom activity are listed below to help you to think about, critically analyse and work towards gender equity. Specific activities from Part Two are referred to, to allow you to explore particular skills.

Generic key questions to explore gender dimensions

Active involvement in group building

- Did any group members dominate the activity? Who? How? 1.7
- Were some group members quiet during the activity? Who? Why? 1.1
- Who took responsibility for the tasks? 1.6?
- Are all children able to participate without being harassed? 1.6

Communication

- Who listened well? 2.10/4.7
- Which group members spoke? 2.1
- Were all voices represented and heard? 2.5
- Which children were unable to verbalise their feelings? 2.5
- What are identifiable cultural differences in terms of communications? 2.1
- How can we cater for different starting points? 2.9
- Were all children's opinions valued? 2.7

Cooperation

Cooperative behavior

- Who were the children who could participate confidently? 2.3/2.8
- Who were the children who were aggressive, assertive and submissive? 2.4/2.8
- Who were the children who were willing to take risks? 3.6/4.4
- How well did children encourage the participation of others? 3.4
- Were all group members' contributions valued? How did children demonstrate this? 3.8

Cooperative roles

- Who were the children who did the tasks such as collecting materials? 3.8
- Who were the children who manipulated materials and/or directed the activities? 3.5

A gender inclusive curriculum

- Who reported/presented group products to the class? 3.1

- Who took responsibility for the allocation of roles and tasks? 2.6/3.4/3.5

- Who took which roles? Are the roles of the group shared around or do some children always take the same roles? Are some roles taken less often (never) by children from particular backgrounds? 3.2

Problem-solving and negotiation

- Did the girls and boys choose to work together? 4.1

- Did children listen to all ideas before making decisions? 4.5

- Were children able to criticise ideas, not people? 4.6

- Were children able to disagree and challenge each other's ideas without resorting to aggression? 4.6

- When there were differences in ideas or opinions, were the children able to negotiate an acceptable decision? 4.5

- Which children made decisions? 4.5

- Who were the children who were key players in negotiating decisions? 4.5

- Did some group members dictate their ideas to the rest of the group? 4.5

- How did children solve conflicts? Were the boys willing to listen? Did the girls assert their own opinions or just give in? 4.1

Planning gender inclusive units of work

Activities which address issues of gender equity should be part of everyday teaching and planned units of work. The questions below are provided as starting points for consideration. There are no simple right and wrong answers. A number of factors will need to be taken into account when making choices about topics, grouping, resources, assessment strategies, etc. The children's prior experiences and beliefs, and skills development, ensuring a balanced curriculum and activity purposes will all influence your decision-making. Ultimately, your selection should be determined by observations and informed reflections — the result of your ongoing monitoring of the learning, children's behavior and your own teaching.

Use these questions as a guide when planning a unit of work and decide for yourself the most appropriate ways to ensure that your program is gender inclusive.

Choosing a topic

- Is the topic relevant and of interest to girls? (How will you know?)
- Does the topic value the traditional and changing lifestyles of women and men?
- Are the contributions of women as well as of men included?
- Are the contributions of women and men from different backgrounds included?
- Will the activity build on girls' knowledge and experience as well as on the boys'? (How will you know?)

Aims and understandings for the topic

- Is there a need to include specific aims which acknowledge different starting points of girls and of boys?
- Do the aims reflect and value the experiences of women and girls a well as men and boys?
- By doing this topic, will the students gain a better understanding about the ways in which gender behaviors are constructed?
- Do the aims include a focus on developing social skills, e.g. active listening, assertive speaking, for all students as well as curriculum content?

Classroom organisation

- What grouping strategy would best cater for all students?
- Will single sex groups be preferable for any activities?
- Would it be appropriate to monitor classroom interactions during the activities to ensure that girls as well as boys receive their share of resources? For example, monitor:
  - how teacher time is spent
  - student groups and roles
  - student behaviors
  - talking/questioning/interruption patterns
  - use of space

A gender inclusive curriculum

- Will cooperative learning strategies be used? How will the roles and tasks be rotated?

Developing new skills

- How can you gauge the skill levels of different girls and boys?
- Will specific skill development be necessary for groups of girls or for groups of boys?
- Will there be opportunities for girls as well as boys to participate in hands-on experiences?
- Will communication and cooperative skills be developed explicitly?
- Do the activities provide challenging opportunities for girls as well as boys?
- Will the activities appeal to all students? (How will you know?)

Teaching strategies

- Will a variety of teaching strategies be used?
- Will the strategies involve all girls and boys?
- How will effective and varied communication among students be encouraged?
- Will cooperative learning be incorporated?
- How will a range of learning areas, e.g. science, literacy, art, mathematics, physical education, be integrated into the unit?
- Will there be an emphasis on practical skills?
- How will positive interactions between children be facilitated?
- Will the girls and boys be involved in making choices about their learning?
- Will the work present women and girls in a positive light?
- How will follow-up questions and discussion draw out and elaborate on the aspects of women presented and why this is important?

Children share and justify their decisions.

Language

- Will there be opportunities to explore the way language works to construct (often limited) understandings of gender 'appropriate' behaviors? (teacher talk, children, texts)

- How will the need to use non-sexist language be addressed?

- Will the language used in this topic turn girls/boys off?

- Do the texts/resources for this topic use non-sexist/inclusive language? If not, how can this be rectified?

Materials and books

- Are any new materials required?

- Will you have enough materials for all students?

- What concrete materials will be used?

A gender inclusive curriculum

- What strategies will ensure that all girls have access to these materials?

- Will the girls/boys have the prerequisite skills to use the materials?

- Will the materials used reflect the interests and experiences of girls as well as boys?

- Does the reference material (fiction and non-fiction):
  - include and value women and girls?
  - portray women and girls positively?
  - include representations of a range of 'masculine' and 'feminine' behaviors?

Assessment and teacher reflections

- Will a variety of assessment and reporting procedures be used, including:
  - descriptive
  - non-competitive
  - peer assessment
  - self-assessment (incorporating student goals)

- How will you as the teacher monitor your own interactions with girls and boys, including:
  - the time spent in disciplining
  - the language used
  - the assumptions you bring to the classroom regarding 'appropriate' behavior for boys/for girls

- How will you involve all students in the planning and evaluation of the teaching and learning program?

- How will you acknowledge and value cooperative behavior within the group?

- How can we best examine our own implicit theory in practice?

[Adapted by A. Allard, M. Cooper, J. Wilson for the VOICES Project 1994. from Planning a work unit to include women and girls in Commonwealth Schools Commission, 1988. *Gender Equity in Mathematics and Science. (GAMAST) Professional Development Manual.* Canberra: Curriculum Development Centre, pp. 57-59.]

Conclusion

This book has explored starting points for teachers who are keen to develop worthwhile interpersonal relationships in the classroom. It considers ways teachers can reflect on their own understandings of gender 'appropriate' behaviors and how these influence interactions with children.

Through an activity-based approach to developing important interpersonal life skills, *Gender Dimensions* aims to enable teachers to teach girls and boys skills crucial for working and learning cooperatively together.

The major focus of this book has been on the work that can be done by teachers and children in individual classrooms. This is an important place of change. We acknowledge that it can be frustrating to realise that other members in the school community do not share our goals of working towards gender equity. Positive work in the classroom to present alternative constructions of masculinity and femininity can be undercut if the rest of the school community rewards only traditional (and limited) constructions of gender.

It is realistic to recognise that steps towards developing more positive relationships among girls and boys work best when the whole school (from principal to cleaner) understands, supports and recognises gender equity as important. It is valuable for teachers, parents and principals to work together to build a whole school community supportive of change. This is an ongoing committment which will have long term results for children.

We encourage teachers to critically examine structures which may exist in schools and to become researchers of their own practice. Teachers are powerful in their own classrooms and they do make a difference in the lives of their children.

Self-assessment

How well did you listen to other group members?

What did you do as a good listener?

How well did other people listen to you?

What did you do as a good speaker?

How did you convey your feelings?

What did you do to ensure that everybody understood?

What did you do to ensure that your team members' feelings were understood?

Peer assessment

Today I observed

....
(insert name and activity observed)

....

....

I noticed

....

....

....

Other comments

....

....

....

Signed .... Date ....

Group assessment

Group members' names: ....

Date: ....

In our group we used these skills

1 ....

2 ....

3 ....

4 ....

5 ....

These are the skills we still need to practise

1 ....

2 ....

3 ....

4 ....

5 ....

Other comments ....

Observation and reflection sheet

Date: ....

Activity: ....

Gender dimensions to observe: ....

....

Student's name	Comments

Teacher considerations/reflections: ....

Blackline Masters 137

Mirroring feelings

A You are feeling hot and tired. Suddenly you smell the most delicious smell imaginable. You look down and there in front of you is a whole plate of freshly baked chocolate chip biscuits. You sit down and enjoy them!

B You are standing in the middle of a beautiful field of flowers enjoying the sunshine and the fragrance. You feel great! However, as you stand there, a dark cloud comes over and suddenly it begins to rain. You are shocked and dismayed by the change in the weather.

C You have just heard the funniest joke ever! You are laughing uncontrollably and having a great time. However, in the midst of your laughter, you look up and suddenly you see the teacher headed straight for you. Oh-oh, you're in trouble now!

D You are waiting at a bus stop and you are in a hurry. As the time goes by, you become more and more anxious and impatient. You will be late for your important game! Where is the bus? When will it come? Slowly your impatience turns to anger and frustration. Now you are really late!

E You pick up the newspaper eagerly looking for the story about your favorite team. There — you find it. But as you read, you discover that the story is insulting to your team. You begin to feel upset and angry. You continue reading and the more you read, the more outraged you feel by what the reporter has to say. What do you do?

F You feel hungry and suddenly you have the idea that you will bake a batch of chocolate biscuits. You gather the ingredients and start mixing them all together. You can't wait to get them in the oven and bake them. Impatiently, you wait while the biscuits bake. You take them out of the oven. They are very hot — but they taste delicious! You feel great.

G You are on your way to school and you feel okay. However, when you look down, you see your dog, Mitsy, has followed you. You stop and tell her to go home. She ignores you and keeps following you. You tell her again. You don't really want to be harsh but she won't listen. You become cross with her and again send her back home. Still she follows you. Now you're going to be late and you feel angry with her.

Blackline Masters

Representing feelings assessment sheet

1 How well did you listen to others?

2 What did you do as a good listener?

3 How well did other people listen to you?

4 What did you do as a good speaker?

5 How well did you convey your feelings?

6 What did you do to ensure that everybody understood?

7 How well did you act as a buddy?

8 How did your buddy feel about your group's feeling word?

9 What did you do to make sure your buddy's feelings were understood?

Talk-up triangle scenarios

- You are the only girl in a group. The boys start telling rude jokes and you are embarrassed. How do you react?

- Your friend borrowed money from you three weeks ago. You need it to buy your mother a birthday present. What do you do?

- You have been waiting for a friend for half an hour. When you get home you ring your friend who says she decided to go out with someone else. What do you say?

- Kids have been teasing/harassing you outside the toilets. How do you react?

- You have been in a queue for ages and your turn comes. When the waiter says 'Who's next?' the boy behind you calls out. What do you do?

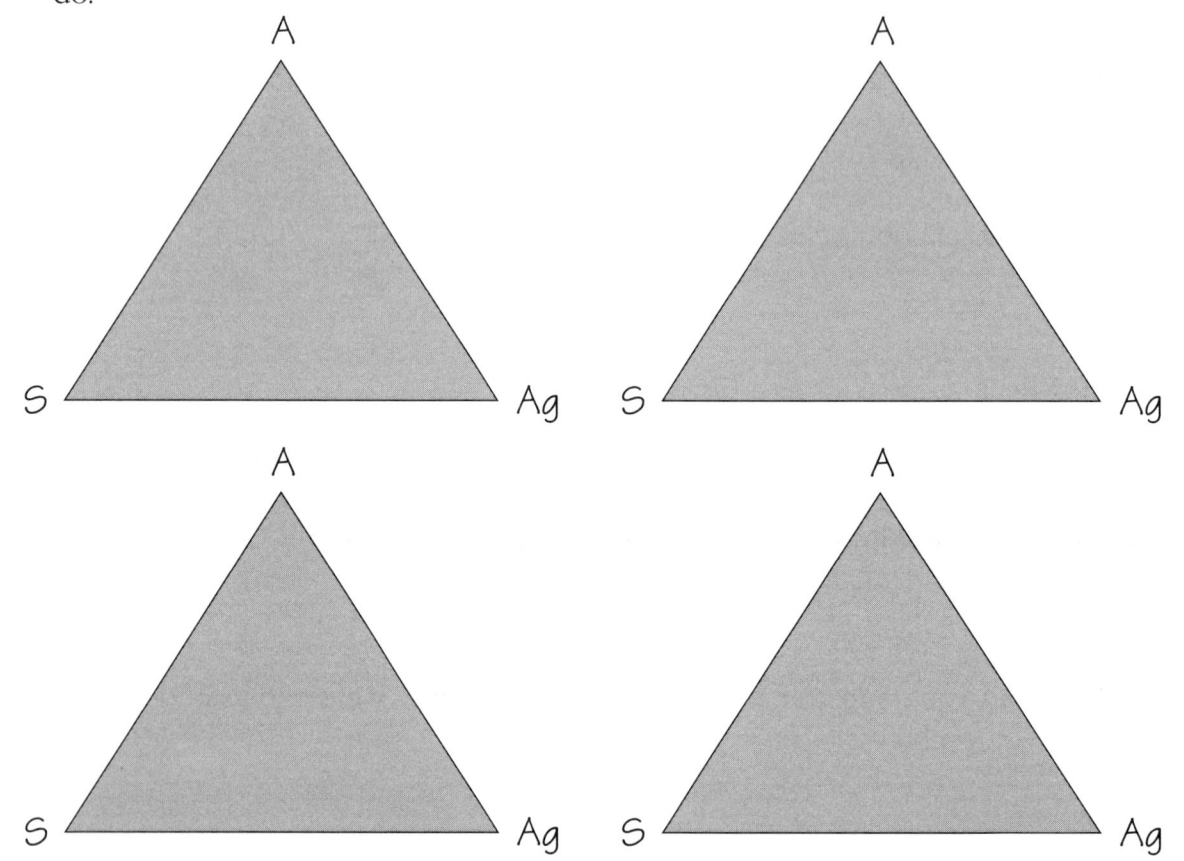

Two-minute controversial responses

It is too time consuming to recycle.

Boys don't need to learn to cook.

Pets should not be allowed within 2 km of native bushland.

Girls can play football and cricket when given the chance.

Unemployed people deserve free housing.

Children should have the right to choose whether they go to school or not.

Good girls always use their manners.

Shops should be open 24 hours a day.

Girls and boys should play together at lunchtime.

Firecrackers should be available at milk bars.

Boys and girls should go to separate schools.

There's a chance

Guess	Clues (counters shown)
1st	
2nd	
3rd	
4th	
5th	
6th	
7th	
8th	
9th	
10th	
11th	
12th	
13th	

Correct combination:

Workers' negotiation

Setting one: Chocolate box factory

Problem: The chocolate box factory has received a large order to make boxes for Valentines Day with a two-day deadline.

Staff involved: The boss, floor manager, union representative and shop floor worker.

Setting two: Telephone book company

Problem: The closing date for placing advertisements has been brought forward a week. There are twenty clients to see.

Staff involved: District manager, sales manager and sales representative and secretary.

Setting three: A country primary school

Problem: The district inspector has been asked to elect a school to sing a song at the opening of a new civic centre.

Staff involved: District inspector, principal, teacher and parent representative.

Setting four: A restaurant

Problem: A busload of overseas tourists has booked into the restaurant and put in a special request for Peking Duck.

Staff involved: Tourist guide, restaurant owner, head waiter and cook.

Setting five: Local council

Problem: A representative from the disabled group has informed the council that the recently installed roundabouts are not suitable for disabled people. They request that all of these be changed.

Staff involved: A representative from the disabled group, council representative, council engineer and council builder.

Blackline Masters

References and bibliography

Adams, C. & Walkerdine, V. 1986, *Investigating Gender Equity in the Primary School: Activity Based Inset Materials for Primary Teachers*, Inner London Education Authority, London.

Allard, A., Bretherton, D. & Collins, L. 1992, *Afters: Gender and Conflict in After School Care Program*, University of Melbourne.

Allard, A., Cooper, M., Hildebrand, G. & Wealands, E. 1995, *STAGES: Steps Towards Addressing Gender in Educational Settings*, Curriculum Corporation, Melbourne.

Australian Education Council 1993, *The National Action Plan For The Education of Girls 1993-1997*, Curriculum Corporation, Melbourne.

Australian Education Council 1992, *Listening to Girls*, Curriculum Corporation, Melbourne.

Baker, J. 1991, *Window*, Julia McCrae, London.

Blackwood, M. & Argent, K. 1987, *Derek the Dinosaur*, Omnibus, Sydney.

Borba, M. & Borba, C. 1978, *Self-Esteem: A Classroom Affair, 101 Ways to Help Children Like Themselves*, vols 1 & 2, Winston Press, Minneapolis.

Carlsson-Paige, N. & Levin, D. 1990, *Who's Calling the Shots? How to Respond Effectively to Children's Fascination with War Play and War Toys*, New Society, Philadelphia.

Chandler, C. 1994, *Dice Don't Have Brains*, MAV, Melbourne.

Clark, M. 1989, *The Great Divide: The Construction of Gender in the Primary School*, Curriculum Development Centre, Canberra.

Commonwealth Schools Commission 1987, *The National Policy for the Education of Girls in Australian Schools*, AGPS, Canberra.

Conflict Resolution Resources for Schools and Youth 1985, *Conflict Managers' Training Manual for Grades 3–6: Starting a Conflict Managers' Program*, Community Board Program Inc., San Francisco.

Connell, R. W. 1987, *Gender and Power*, Allen & Unwin, Sydney.

Connor, G. 1988, *Self-Esteem: Teachers Hold Some Keys. A resource supporting social development and self-esteem in schools*, Ministry of Education, Perth.

Cornelius, H. & Faire, S. 1989, *Everyone Can Win: How To Resolve Conflict*, Simon & Schuster, Sydney.

Curriculum Development Centre 1987, *Including Girls: Curriculum Perspectives on the Education of Girls*, Commonwealth Schools Commission, Canberra.

Dalton, J. 1985, *Adventures in Thinking: Creative Thinking and Cooperative Talk in Small Groups*, Nelson, Melbourne.

Davies, B. 1989, *Frogs and Snails and Feminist Tales*, Allen & Unwin, Sydney.

Davies, B. 1993, *Shards of Glass*, Allen & Unwin, Sydney.

Directorate of School Education 1993, *I Spy Technology: Practical Ideas for Gender Equity in Primary Technology Studies*, DSE, Melbourne.

Dyson, S. & Szirom, T. 1989, *Far, Far Greater Things: A Source Book for Women's Groups*, YWCA, Melbourne.

Gilbert, P. 1987, 'Beware the innocent stories of children', *Curriculum Development in Australian Schools*, no. 3, January, pp. 22–3.

Gilbert, P. 1989a, *Writing, Schooling and Deconstruction: From Voice to Text in the Classroom*, Routledge, London.

Gilbert, P. 1989b, 'Personally (and passively) yours: Girls, literacy and education', *Oxford Review of Education*, vol. 15, no. 3, pp. 257-65.

Gilbert, P. & Rowe, K. 1989, *Gender, Literacy and the Classroom*, ARA, Canberra.

Gilligan, C. 1982, *In a Different Voice: Psychological Theory and Women's Development*, Harvard University Press, Cambridge, Mass.

Gilligan, C., Ward, J. & Taylor, J. 1988, *Mapping the Moral Domain*, Center for the Study of Gender, Education and Human Development, Harvard University, Cambridge, Mass.

Hancock, K. & Blaby, B. 1989, *People Interacting: Self-Awareness, Communication, Social Skills and Problem Solving*, Nelson, Melbourne.

Harding, J. 1984, 'Values, cognitive style and the curriculum', in *Contributions to the Third International Girls and Science and Technology Conference (GASAT) 3*, London.

Harding, J. 1985, *Switch Off: The Science Education of Girls*, Longman, London.

Hill, S. & Hill, T. 1990, *The Collaborative Classroom: A Guide to Co-operative Learning*, Eleanor Curtain, Melbourne.

Hill, S. 1992, *Games That Work: Co-operative Games and Activities for the Primary School Classroom*, Eleanor Curtain, Melbourne.

Hilton, N. 1987, *The Long Red Scarf*, Omnibus, Sydney.

Hlebowitsch, P. & Tellez, K. 1993, 'Pre-service teachers and their students: Early views of race, gender and class', *Journal of Education for Teaching*, vol. 19, no. 1, pp. 41-51.

Inclusive Curriculum Technological Studies Project, Participation & Equity Program 1987, *Made to Measure: Issues of Teaching Technology to Girls and Boys*, Ministry of Education, Melbourne.

Ingpen, R. & Dunkle, M. 1986, *Conservation*, Penguin, Melbourne.

Jones, A. 1989, 'The cultural production of classroom practice', *British Journal of Sociology of Education*, vol. 10, no. 1, pp. 19-31.

Kneidler, W. J. 1984, *Gender Equity in Mathematics and Science*, Curriculum Development Centre, Canberra.

Kotzman, A. 1989, *Listen to Me, Listen to You*, Penguin, Harmondsworth.

Kroehnert, G. 1991, *100 Training Games*, McGraw Hill, Sydney.

Mac an Ghaill, M. 1994, *The Making of Men: Masculinities, Sexualities and Schooling*, Open University Press, Philadelphia.

McClintock Collective 1988, *Getting Into Gear: Gender Inclusive Teaching Strategies in Science*, Curriculum Development Centre, Canberra.

McGrath, H. & Francey, S. 1991, *Friendly Kids, Friendly Classrooms*, Longman, Melbourne.

Munch, R. 1980, *The Paperbag Princess*, Pinnacle Press, Toronto.

Murdoch, K. 1992, *Integrating Naturally*, Dellasta, Melbourne.

NESB Girls & Computers Project Team 1987, *Switch It On, Miss! A Project Investigating Computer Technology and Its Relevance to the Education of Ethnic Minority Girls*, Ministerial Advisory Committee on Multicultural and Migrant Education and State Computer Education Centre, Melbourne.

Prutzman, P. 1978, *Friendly Classroom for a Small Planet*, New Society, Philadelphia

Reid, J., Forrestal, P. & Cook, J. 1989, *Small Group Learning in the Classroom*, PETA, Perth.

Sadker, M. and Sadker, D. 1982, *Sex Equity Handbook for Schools*, Longman, New York.

Slavin, R. 1985, *Learning to Cooperate, Cooperating to Learn*, Plenum Press, New York.

Sobel. J. 1983, *Everybody Wins*, Walker & Co., New York.

Spender, D. and Sarah, E. (eds) 1980, *Learning to Lose: Sexism in Education*, The Women's Press, London.

Swartz, V., Allard, A. & Matthews, B. 1989, *A Fair Go For All: Guidelines for a Gender-inclusive Curriculum*, Office of Schools Administration, Ministry of Education, Melbourne.

Tsolidis, G. 1986, *Educating Voula: A Report on Non-English Speaking Background Girls and Education*, Ministry of Education Ministerial Advisory Committee on Multicultural and Migrant Education and State Computer Education Centre, Melbourne.

Weiler, K. 1988, 'Gender, race, and class in the feminist classroom' in K. Weiler (ed.), *Women Teaching for Change: Gender, Class and Power*. Bergin & Garvey, Boston, Mass.

Weinstein, M. & Goodman, J. 1980, *Playfair: Everybody's Guide to Noncompetitive Play*, Impact, San Jose, Cal.

Wilson, J. & Allard, A. 1993, 'You can't play because you're a girl: What girls know about gender issues', *Primary Education*, April.

Wilson, J. & Egeberg, P. 1990, *Cooperative Challenges and Student Investigations*, Nelson, Melbourne.

Wilson, J. & Hollingsworth, H. 1993, *Springboards: Ideas for Maths*, Nelson, Melbourne.

Wilson, J. & Hoyne, P. 1993, *Cooperative Challenges for Infants*, Nelson, Melbourne.

Wilson, J. and Wing Jan, L. 1993, *Thinking for Themselves: Developing Strategies for Reflective Learning*, Eleanor Curtain, Melbourne.

Wyn, J. 1990, 'Working class girls and educational outcomes', in J. Kenway & S. Willis (eds), *Hearts and Minds: Self Esteem and the Schooling of Girls*, Falmer Press, Barcombe, UK.

Index

active listening 9, 44–5
   activities 58–73
   moving forward 75–7
   and negotiation 103
activities
   active listening 58–63
   assertive speaking 64–73
   cooperative learning 82–99
   group building 26–39
   non-verbal communication 44–55
   overview and layout 22–3
   problem-solving and negotiation 104–21
advertising and gendered expectations 87–9
aggression v. assertion 69
'appropriate' behaviors 4, 15
   see also gender beliefs
assertion 69
   v. aggression 46, 66–9
   v. submission 66–9
assertive speaking 9–10, 45, 64–73
   and ethnicity 47
   moving forward 78–9
   and negotiation 103
assessment 132
assumptions 2

caring for others 104–7
classroom organisation 129
collaboration 98–9

communication 9–11, 43–7
   active listening 9, 44–5
   activities 48–73
   assertive speaking 9–10, 45–7
   key questions 127
   non-verbal 9, 43–4
   and teaching skills 17
   what boys say 11
   what girls say 10–11
compliments 34–5
conflict resolution 72–3
consensus decisions 96–7
constructive learning environments 2
   beliefs 14
   elements of 7–14
   and skills 7–8
cooperation 11–13
   key questions 127–8
cooperative learning 80–1
   activities 80–99
   allocating roles 81, 90
   and ethnicity 81
   moving forward 100–2
   and negotiation 103
   and teaching skills 18
   what boys say 12–13
   what girls say 11–12
counter-sexist stories 84–6
creativity and imagination 118–19
curriculum planning and gender inclusive activities 128–32

developing new skills 130

empathy 52–3, 58–9
equity 2–3
ethnicity
    and assertive speaking 47
    and cooperative learning 81
    and gender 16
    and non-verbal communication 44

fairy stories, traditional roles 84–6
feelings
    and emotions 60–1
    expressing non-verbally 32–3

gender beliefs 6, 32
    and active listening 45
    challenging 108–11
    and conflict 72
    and cooperative learning 80, 90
    and ethnicity 16
    and group building 24
    influences on teaching 3, 4, 15–16
    making explicit 16
    and non-verbal communication 43, 48
    and public speaking 70
    traditional fairy stories 84–6
giving directions 62–3, 64–5
group building 8–9, 24–5
    activities 26–39
    key questions 127
    moving forward 40–2
    skill development 40–2
    and teaching skills 17
group cohesiveness 94–5

'I' statements 46, 66–9

language 131
    and behavior 5
listening skills, non-verbal 48–9

materials and resources 131
moving forward
    active listening 75–7
    assertive speaking 78–9
    cooperative learning 100–2
    group building 40–2
    non-verbal communication 74–5
    problem-solving and negotiation 122–4

negotiation 13–14, 120–1
    see also problem-solving and negotiation
non-verbal communication 9, 43–4
    activities 48–55
    and ethnicity 44
    expressing feelings 32
    making skills explicit 44
    moving forward 74–5
non-verbal listening skills 48–9

positive self-image 26–7, 38–9
problem-solving and negotiation 13–14, 103
    activities 104–121
    key questions 128
    moving forward 122–4
    and teaching skills 18–19
public speaking 70–1

risk-taking 30–1, 112–13, 114–15
role allocation and cooperative groups 90–1, 92–3

self-awareness 38–9
self-confidence 36–7
self-image 26–7, 38–9
sex v. gender 6
skill development 6, 7–8, 130
skills, making explicit 44
social issues 116–17
social skills 28–9
social structures 5–6
stereotypes 108–11
submission v. assertion 69

teacher reflection 132
teachers as learners 16–20
teaching strategies 130
teaching
    and gender beliefs 16–19
    working towards change 20
team work 54–7, 82–3
terminology 6
topic selection 129

valuing differences 4–5, 108–11
valuing women and girls 3–4

Other books from Eleanor Curtain

Book Talk
Collaborative Responses to Literature

Susan Hill & Jane O'Loughlin

Book Talk presents dozens of exciting collaborative structures which generate ideas for discussion and encourage a deeper involvement with books and literature. These activities encourage the many genres of talk as well as a variety of written responses: recounting ideas, creating narratives, describing details, explaining a point of view, creating arguments to define a position. The activities are suitable for a broad range of students and have been used with students from five to eighteen years of age.

ISBN 1 875327 33 9   Illustrated 96 pp

Games That Work
Co-operative Games and Activities for the Primary School Classroom

Susan Hill

This practical resource presents games and activities to engage children, and to introduce them to the idea and the practice of collaboration. *Games That Work* focuses on communication and co-operation, the underpinning of all learning. The features of collaboration are made explicit and the games are presented not as isolated activities, but as preparation and structuring for group work.

Contents:
- Elements of co-operative learning — shared goals, positive interdependence
- Forming group games — getting acquainted; mixing it up; pairs and partners
- Working as a group — games, activities, roles
- Games and activities for problem solving — for managing differences
- Games for big spaces

ISBN 1 875327 16 9   Illustrated 128 pp

Pathways to Co-operation
Starting Points for Co-operative Learning
Dot Walker and Pamela Brown

Pathways to Co-operation identifies eight 'ways in' or pathways which act as starting points to establishing a collaborative classroom: recognition of and accommodation of difference, implementation of child-centred programs, providing constructive feedback, providing for reflection, empowering children as learners, acknowledging that metacognition is an optimum level for thinking and learning , celebrating learning and providing for quality communication.

Pathways to Co-operation is a flexible resource which provides a wide range of games, activities and strategies. The large format and wealth of illustrative material makes the information accessible and the book enjoyable to use.

ISBN 1 875327 20 7   Illustrated 128 pp

Peace in the Classroom
Practical Lessons in Living for Elementary Age Children
Hetty Adams

This thought-provoking book is a complete peace education program, organised into six thematic units. It is full of practical, enjoyable, open-ended activities that can be used alone, extended and enhanced to become mini-themes, or integrated with other curricular areas such as language, social studies and art. Each lesson has an objective, list of materials needed, instructions and questions teachers can use to encourage classroom discussion.

ISBN 1 895411 68 8   Illustrated 144 pp

Developing Thinking Skills
Using Children's Literature
Ann and Johnny Baker

Developing Thinking Skills uses picture story books to introduce children to a range of thinking skills. Picture books arouse the curiosity and stimulate the imagination of children; they pose challenges and problem situations; they provide a safe context in which children can explore a range of outcomes to a possible situation.

Developing Thinking Skills introduces thinking as part of a worthwhile activity and in a meaningful context. The thinking skills and activities are integrated across the curriculum and the thinking itself is made explicit by using the related language to describe the processes and outcomes. Reflection time is built into the process.

ISBN 1 875327 24 X   Illustrated 96 pp

Making Themes Work

Anne Davies, Colleen Politano and Caren Cameron

Making Themes Work shows teachers how to organise curriculum and effectively integrate learning experiences using themes. In *Making Themes Work*, you'll find many valuable examples and strategies, including innovative ways to start a theme; effective ways for students to show what they know; practical ways to think about theme planning; powerful evaluation strategies; classroom-tested ways to manage and organise themes; common questions about themes — and the answers; ways to inform parents, administrators and colleagues about learning through themes.

ISBN 1-895411-60-2   Illustrated 88 pp

Multi-Age and More

Colleen Politano and Anne Davies

Every classroom is a multi-age classroom; even same-age students have varied skills, abilities and interests. *Multi-Age and More* is for all teachers who are looking for ways to meet the challenges of the diverse learning needs of their students.

Multi-Age and More provides teachers with practical strategies for managing and teaching any multi-age, multi-ability and multi-interest class: to plan, organise and modify the curriculum, to get students to show you what they know, to make assessment and evaluation an integral part of learning and teaching, to use available physical space and materials effectively, to work with parents, colleagues and school educators.

Anne Davies and Colleen Politano are also co-authors of *Together Is Better: Collaborative Assessment, Evaluation and Reporting*

ISBN 1-895411-65-3   Illustrated 160 pp

Journals in the Classroom
A Complete Guide for the Elementary Teacher

Janine Brodine and Judith Issacs

In *Journals in the Classroom*, the authors discuss how journal writing promotes fluency and instils confidence through writing. They explain how to integrate all types of journals — individual, dialogue, buddy and team journals, learning logs — into classroom curriculum. Journaling techniques, such as free writing, clustering, altered point of view, unsent letters and maps, are explored. A chapter on integrating journals into all content areas, a question-and-answer section, and dozens of actual work samples make this a comprehensive resource.

ISBN 1 895411 69 6   Illustrated 144 pp

Reading and Writing Communities
Co-operative Literacy Learning in the Classroom
Susan Hill and Joelie Hancock

Co-operative learning, a way to organise and structure classroom experience, has immense potential for improving the way children learn. The links between co-operation and communication form a powerful base for learning in all subject areas. *Reading and Writing Communities* presents guidelines, case studies and practical activities for creating a powerful reading and writing community within the classroom.

Contents include:
- Achieving gains in performance and achievement
- Literature and the wider community
- Building cohesion: creating the classroom culture
- Co-operative learning and literacy
- Setting and meeting goals in reading
- Setting and meeting goals in writing
- Feedback, evaluation and goal setting.

ISBN 1 875327 12 6   Illustrated 128 pp

Readers Theatre
Performing the Text
Susan Hill

Readers Theatre presents a simple, informal and motivating way to involve students in the study of literature by group story-telling, shared reading, improvisation and performance of a favourite story. *Readers Theatre* provides: complete scripts for performance, guide-lines for helping children write their own scripts, aids and ideas for improvisation, lists of texts that work well in adaptation.

ISBN 1 875327 01 0   Illustrated 88 pp

Jump for Joy
More Raps & Rhymes
Susan Hill

Jump for Joy is the exciting successor to Susan Hill's *Raps & Rhymes*, which is so popular in classrooms throughout Australia and has become an instant hit with teachers and children in the USA, Canada and New Zealand. *Jump for Joy* provides a variety of chants and poems for reading aloud selected with an eye to fun as well as learning.

Contents include: Claps and Clicks, Games and Actions, Chants with Two Parts, Chants with More Voices, Absolute Nonsense.

ISBN 1 875327 17 7   Illustrated 64 pp

Raps & Rhymes
Selected by Susan Hill

Raps & Rhymes is a stimulating selection of traditional chants and rhymes that have been played with, improvised on and read by children of all ages. Reading aloud as a group, joining in a chant or a rhyme is a great warm-up to any lesson, and an effective way to build up a feeling of cohesiveness in class.

Contents include:

Improvising, Clapping and Clicking, Action Rhymes, Part-reading and Nonsense

ISBN 1 875327 03 7   Illustrated 80 pp